# The Rules of Golf

# The Rules of Golf

*as approved by*
*The United States Golf Association®*
*and*
*The Royal and Ancient Golf Club*
*of St. Andrews, Scotland*

*Effective January 1, 2000*

**TRIUMPH**
BOOKS
CHICAGO

Typographer: Sue Knopf

For more information on the USGA®, contact:

United States Golf Association
Golf House
Far Hills, NJ 07931

The USGA On-Line
Join the USGA on the Internet at http://www.usga.org

This book is available in quantity at special discounts for your group
or organization.

**For further information, contact:**

Triumph Books
601 South LaSalle Street, Suite 500
Chicago, Illinois 60605
Tel (312) 939-3330
Fax (312) 663-3557

# How to Use the Rules Book

**UNDERSTAND THE WORDS**

The Rules book is written in a very precise and deliberate fashion. You should be aware of and understand the following differences in word use.

| | | |
|---|---|---|
| May | = | optional |
| Should | = | recommendation |
| Shall/must | = | instruction (and penalty if not carried out) |
| A ball | = | you may substitute another ball (e.g. Rules 26, 27 or 28) |
| The ball | = | you may not substitute another ball (e.g. Rules 24-2 or 25-1) |

**KNOW THE DEFINITIONS**

There are over forty defined terms and these form the foundation around which the Rules of play are written. A good knowledge of the defined terms (which are italicized throughout the book) is very important to the correct application of the Rules.

**WHICH RULE APPLIES?**

The Contents pages may help you find the relevant Rule; alternatively there is an Index at the back of the book.

**WHAT IS THE RULING?**

To answer any question on the Rules you must first establish the facts of the case.

To do so, you should identify:

1. The form of play (e.g. match play or stroke play, single, four-some or four-ball?)
2. Who is involved (e.g. the player, his partner or caddie, an outside agency?)
3. Where the incident occurred (e.g. on the teeing ground, in a bunker or water hazard, on the putting green or elsewhere on the course).

In some cases it might also be necessary to establish:

4. The player's intentions (e.g. what was he doing and what does he want to do?)
5. Any subsequent events (e.g. the player has returned his score card or the competition has closed).

## REFER TO THE BOOK

It is recommended that you carry a Rules book in your golf bag and use it whenever a question arises. If in doubt, play the course as you find it and play the ball as it lies. Once back in the Clubhouse, reference to "Decisions on the Rules of Golf" should help resolve any outstanding queries.

# FOREWORD

The United States Golf Association and the Royal and Ancient Golf Club of St. Andrews, in consultation with other golfing bodies from throughout the world, have carried out their customary quadrennial review of the Rules of Golf and have adopted this new code, which is effective from January 1, 2000.

As in previous years, substantive changes have been kept to a minimum, but a number of Rules have been amended or re-drafted in continuance of the policy of making the Rules of Golf as clear as possible. In addition, Appendix I relating to Local Rules and Conditions of Competition, has been re-written in an attempt to help Committees deal with local abnormal conditions and establish appropriate competition conditions. The principal changes are summarized on the following three pages.

The United States Golf Association and the Royal and Ancient Golf Club of St. Andrews will continue their close liaison in all matters concerning the Rules and their respective and mutual efforts to preserve and enhance the integrity of the game and its Rules. Both organizations would like to record their appreciation of the valuable assistance which they have received from other golfing bodies throughout the world.

We take this opportunity of thanking, most sincerely, our respective Committees and all who have helped us in our endeavors.

Reed K. Mackenzie
Chairman
Rules of Golf Committee
United States Golf Association

David I. Pepper
Chairman
Rules of Golf Committee
Royal and Ancient Golf Club
    of St. Andrews

# *Changes Since 1998*

## DEFINITIONS

### Ground Under Repair

Amended to state that a ball off the ground but in a bush or tree rooted in ground under repair is in ground under repair.

### Nearest Point of Relief

A new Definition to reflect the recommended procedure for determining the nearest point of relief from an 'immovable obstruction,' an 'abnormal ground condition' and a 'wrong putting green.'

## RULES

### Rule 4. Clubs

Previously the Rules on clubs were contained in Rule 4 and Appendix II. The specifications on clubs have been re-positioned in Appendix II and Rule 4 restructured accordingly.

### Rule 4-3. Damage

A new Rule to consolidate all references to a damaged club (previously Rules 4-1g, 4-2 and 4-4a referred) and to clarify the player's options when a club is damaged.

### Rule 6-8. Discontinuance of Play

Rule 6-8c has been amended to state that a player may lift his ball without penalty only if the Committee has suspended play or there is a good reason to lift it. Rule 6-8d has been added to clarify the procedure when play is resumed.

### Rule 13-2. Improving Lie, Area of Intended Stance or Swing, or Line of Play

Expanded to cover the improvement of the area of the player's intended stance and the prohibited actions to include removing dew, frost or water.

### Rule 14-2. Assistance

Amended to state that a player must not allow his caddie, partner or partner's caddie to stand on or close to an extension of the 'line of play' or 'line of putt' behind the ball while he is making a stroke anywhere on the course. Previously, this prohibition was limited to the putting green under Rule 16-1, which has been restructured accordingly.

### Rule 14-3. Artificial Devices and Unusual Equipment

The permission to apply tape or gauze to a grip during a stipulated round, other than for repair, has been withdrawn to eliminate the conflict between this Rule and Rule 4-2 which prohibits changing the playing characteristics of a club during the stipulated round.

## Rule 20-2c. Dropping and Re-Dropping

Clause (vii) has been amended to include reference to the 'nearest point of relief' and the point of maximum available relief. Therefore, a dropped ball must be re-dropped if it rolls and comes to rest nearer the hole than these points.

## Rule 24-2b. Immovable Obstruction

Amended to incorporate the new Definition of Nearest Point of Relief. Also, the prohibition against crossing over, through or under the obstruction in determining the 'nearest point of relief' has been eliminated, except that a Committee may re-introduce such a prohibition by Local Rule when the nature of a particular obstruction would warrant it.

## Rule 24-2c. Immovable Obstruction—Ball Lost

Amended to state that if a ball is lost in an immovable obstruction, the ball is deemed to lie at the spot where it last entered the obstruction and Rule 24-2b is then applied in relation to a ball so positioned.

## Rule 25-1b. Abnormal Ground Conditions

Amended to incorporate the new Definitions of Abnormal Ground Conditions, Burrowing Animal and Nearest Point of Relief. The consolidation of the relief procedures has been made possible by denying relief from ground under repair in a water hazard.

Also, the relief procedure in a bunker has been amended so that if complete relief is available, the player may lift the ball and drop it within one club-length of the 'nearest point of relief.' It will be only if complete relief is not possible that the player will drop the ball at the nearest point of maximum available relief (i.e., without a one club-length dropping area).

## Rule 25-1c. Abnormal Ground Conditions—Ball Lost

Amended for clarity and consistency with Rule 24-2c.

## Rule 27. Ball Lost or Out of Bounds; Provisional Ball

Amended for clarity.

## Rule 32-1. Bogey, Par and Stableford Competitions

A Note has been added to Rules 32-1a and 32-1b to clarify the penalty for a breach of Rule 6-7 (Undue Delay; Slow Play).

## Rule 33-2d. The Course—Course Unplayable

The reference to resumption of play has been deleted; see Rule 6-8d.

## APPENDIX I

**Local Rules and Conditions of Competition**

Substantially amended to create an Appendix which is the same in the R&A's and the USGA's Rules books. The principal changes are the inclusion of sections on, and recommended wordings of Local Rules for, Environmentally-Sensitive Areas and Temporary Obstructions. Also, there is an expanded section on Preferred Lies and new sections on How to Decide Ties and Draws for Match Play.

## APPENDIX II

**Design of Clubs**

Substantially amended and restructured to incorporate the specifications previously contained in Rule 4. Other principal changes include:

- the adjustability clause (Clause 1.b) is amended for clarity.
- the clause concerning 'spring-like' effect (Clause 5.a) refers to a new test protocol.

## APPENDIX III

**The Ball**

Re-numbered for consistency with Appendix II.

Also, the specifications in the Rules on Initial Velocity and Overall Distance have been deleted. However, in effect, neither the Rules nor their interpretation have been changed as the specifications have been re-positioned in the appropriate test protocols kept on file.

# Contents

## Teeing Ground

## Playing the Ball

## The Putting Green

## Ball Moved, Deflected or Stopped

## Relief Situations and Procedure

# SECTION I
# *ETIQUETTE*

## *Courtesy on the Course*

### Safety

Prior to playing a *stroke* or making a practice swing, the player should ensure that no one is standing close by or in a position to be hit by the club, the ball or any stones, pebbles, twigs or the like which may be moved by the *stroke* or swing.

### Consideration for Other Players

The player who has the *honor* should be allowed to play before his opponent or *fellow-competitor* tees his ball.

No one should move, talk or stand close to or directly behind the ball or the *hole* when a player is *addressing the ball* or making a *stroke*.

No player should play until the players in front are out of range.

### Pace of Play

In the interest of all, players should play without delay.

If a player believes his ball may be *lost* outside a *water hazard* or *out of bounds,* to save time, he should play a *provisional ball*.

Players searching for a ball should signal the players behind them to pass as soon as it becomes apparent that the ball will not easily be found. They should not search for five minutes before doing so. They should not continue play until the players following them have passed and are out of range.

When the play of a hole has been completed, players should immediately leave the *putting green*.

If a match fails to keep its place on the *course* and loses

---

more than one clear hole on the players in front, it should invite the match following to pass.

## *Priority on the Course*

In the absence of special rules, two-ball *matches* should have precedence over and be entitled to pass any three- or four-ball *match*, which should invite them through.

A single player has no standing and should give way to a *match* of any kind.

Any *match* playing a whole round is entitled to pass a *match* playing a shorter round.

## *Care of the Course*

### Holes in Bunkers

Before leaving a *bunker*, a player should carefully fill up and smooth over all holes and footprints made by him.

### Repair Divots, Ball-Marks and Damage by Spikes

A player should ensure that any divot hole made by him and any damage to the *putting green* made by a ball is carefully repaired. On completion of the hole by all players in the group, damage to the *putting green* caused by golf shoe spikes should be repaired.

### Damage to Greens—Flagsticks, Bags, etc.

Players should ensure that, when putting down bags or the *flagstick*, no damage is done to the *putting green* and that neither they nor their *caddies* damage the *hole* by standing close to it, in handling the *flagstick* or in removing the ball from the *hole*. The *flagstick* should be properly replaced in the *hole* before the players leave the *putting green*. Players should not damage the *putting green* by leaning on their putters, particularly when removing the ball from the *hole*.

**Golf Carts**

Local notices regulating the movement of golf carts should be strictly observed.

**Damage Through Practice Swings**

In taking practice swings, players should avoid causing damage to the *course*, particularly the tees, by removing divots.

# Section II
## *DEFINITIONS*

## Abnormal Ground Conditions

An *"abnormal ground condition"* is any *casual water*, *ground under repair* or hole, cast or runway on the *course* made by a *burrowing animal*, a reptile or a bird.

## Addressing the Ball

A player has *"addressed the ball"* when he has taken his *stance* and has also grounded his club, except that in a *hazard* a player has *addressed the ball* when he has taken his *stance*.

## Advice

*"Advice"* is any counsel or suggestion which could influence a player in determining his play, the choice of a club or the method of making a *stroke*.

Information on the *Rules* or on matters of public information, such as the position of *hazards* or the *flagstick* on the *putting green*, is not *advice*.

## Ball Deemed to Move

See *"Move or Moved."*

## Ball Holed

See *"Holed."*

## Ball Lost

See *"Lost Ball."*

## Ball in Play

A ball is *"in play"* as soon as the player has made a *stroke* on the *teeing ground*. It remains *in play* until *holed* out, except when it is *lost*, *out of bounds* or lifted, or another ball has been substituted whether or not such substitution is permitted; a ball so substituted becomes the ball *in play*.

## Bunker

A *"bunker"* is a *hazard* consisting of a prepared area of ground, often a hollow, from which turf or soil has been removed and replaced with sand or the like. Grass-covered ground bordering or within a *bunker* is not part of the *bunker*. The margin of a *bunker* extends vertically downwards, but not upwards. A ball is in a *bunker* when it lies in or any part of it touches the *bunker*.

## Burrowing Animals

A *"burrowing animal"* is an animal that makes a hole for habitation or shelter, such as a rabbit, mole, ground hog, gopher or salamander.

**Note:** A hole made by a non-burrowing animal, such as a dog, is not an *abnormal ground condition* unless marked or declared as *ground under repair*.

## Caddie

A *"caddie"* is one who carries or handles a player's clubs during play and otherwise assists him in accordance with the *Rules*.

When one *caddie* is employed by more than one player, he is always deemed to be the *caddie* of the player whose ball is involved, and *equipment* carried by him is deemed to be that player's *equipment*, except when the *caddie* acts upon specific directions of another player, in which case he is considered to be that other player's *caddie*.

## Casual Water

*"Casual water"* is any temporary accumulation of water on the *course* which is visible before or after the player takes his *stance* and is not in a *water hazard*. Snow and natural ice, other than frost, are either *casual water* or *loose impediments*, at the option of the player. Manufactured

ice is an *obstruction*. Dew and frost are not *casual water*. A ball is in *casual water* when it lies in or any part of it touches the *casual water*.

## Committee

The *"Committee"* is the committee in charge of the competition or, if the matter does not arise in a competition, the committee in charge of the *course*.

## Competitor

A *"competitor"* is a player in a stroke competition. A *"fellow-competitor"* is any person with whom the *competitor* plays. Neither is *partner* of the other.

In stroke play foursome and four-ball competitions, where the context so admits, the word *"competitor"* or *"fellow-competitor"* includes his *partner*.

## Course

The *"course"* is the whole area within which play is permitted (see Rule 33-2).

## Equipment

*"Equipment"* is anything used, worn or carried by or for the player except any ball he has played at the hole being played and any small object, such as a coin or a tee, when used to mark the position of a ball or the extent of an area in which a ball is to be dropped. *Equipment* includes a golf cart, whether or not motorized. If such a cart is shared by two or more players, the cart and everything in it are deemed to be the *equipment* of the player whose ball is involved except that, when the cart is being moved by one of the players sharing it, the cart and everything in it are deemed to be that player's *equipment*.

**Note:** A ball played at the hole being played is *equipment* when it has been lifted and not put back into play.

**Fellow-Competitor**

See *"Competitor."*

**Flagstick**

The *"flagstick"* is a movable straight indicator, with or without bunting or other material attached, centered in the *hole* to show its position. It shall be circular in cross-section.

**Forecaddie**

A *"forecaddie"* is one who is employed by the *Committee* to indicate to players the position of balls during play. He is an *outside agency*.

**Ground Under Repair**

*"Ground under repair"* is any part of the *course* so marked by order of the *Committee* or so declared by its authorized representative. It includes material piled for removal and a hole made by a greenkeeper, even if not so marked.

All ground and any grass, bush, tree or other growing thing within the *ground under repair* is part of the *ground under repair*. The margin of *ground under repair* extends vertically downwards, but not upwards. Stakes and lines defining *ground under repair* are in such ground. Such stakes are *obstructions*. A ball is in *ground under repair* when it lies in or any part of it touches the *ground under repair*.

**Note 1:** Grass cuttings and other material left on the *course* which have been abandoned and are not intended to be removed are not *ground under repair* unless so marked.

**Note 2:** The *Committee* may make a Local Rule prohibiting play from *ground under repair* or an environmentally-sensitive area which has been defined as *ground under repair.*

### Hazards

A *"hazard"* is any *bunker* or *water hazard.*

### Hole

The *"hole"* shall be 4¼ inches (108mm) in diameter and at least 4 inches (100mm) deep. If a lining is used, it shall be sunk at least 1 inch (25mm) below the *putting green* surface unless the nature of the soil makes it impracticable to do so; its outer diameter shall not exceed 4¼ inches (108mm).

### Holed

A ball is *"holed"* when it is at rest within the circumference of the *hole* and all of it is below the level of the lip of the *hole.*

### Honor

The player who is to play first from the *teeing ground* is said to have the *"honor."*

### Lateral Water Hazard

A *"lateral water hazard"* is a *water hazard* or that part of a *water hazard* so situated that it is not possible or is deemed by the *Committee* to be impracticable to drop a ball behind the *water hazard* in accordance with Rule 26-1b.

That part of a *water hazard* to be played as a *lateral water hazard* should be distinctively marked. A ball is in a *lateral water hazard* when it lies in or any part of it touches the *lateral water hazard.*

**Note 1:** *Lateral water hazards* should be defined by red stakes or lines.

**Note 2:** The *Committee* may make a Local Rule prohibiting play from an environmentally-sensitive area which has been defined as a *lateral water hazard*.

**Note 3:** The *Committee* may define a *lateral water hazard* as a *water hazard*.

### Line of Play

The *"line of play"* is the direction which the player wishes his ball to take after a *stroke*, plus a reasonable distance on either side of the intended direction. The *line of play* extends vertically upwards from the ground, but does not extend beyond the *hole*.

### Line of Putt

The *"line of putt"* is the line which the player wishes his ball to take after a *stroke* on the *putting green*. Except with respect to Rule 16-1e, the *line of putt* includes a reasonable distance on either side of the intended line. The *line of putt* does not extend beyond the *hole*.

### Loose Impediments

*"Loose impediments"* are natural objects such as stones, leaves, twigs, branches and the like, dung, worms and insects and casts or heaps made by them, provided they are not fixed or growing, are not solidly embedded and do not adhere to the ball.

Sand and loose soil are *loose impediments* on the *putting green*, but not elsewhere.

Snow and natural ice, other than frost, are either *casual water* or *loose impediments*, at the option of the player. Manufactured ice is an *obstruction*.

Dew and frost are not *loose impediments*.

## Lost Ball

A ball is *"lost"* if:

a. It is not found or identified as his by the player within five minutes after the player's *side* or his or their *caddies* have begun to search for it; or

b. The player has put another ball into play under the *Rules*, even though he may not have searched for the original ball; or

c. The player has played any *stroke* with a *provisional ball* from the place where the original ball is likely to be or from a point nearer the *hole* than that place, whereupon the *provisional ball* becomes the *ball in play*.

Time spent in playing a *wrong ball* is not counted in the five-minute period allowed for search.

## Marker

A *"marker"* is one who is appointed by the *Committee* to record a *competitor's* score in stroke play. He may be a *fellow-competitor*. He is not a *referee*.

## Matches

See *"Sides and Matches."*

## Move or Moved

A ball is deemed to have *"moved"* if it leaves its position and comes to rest in any other place.

## Nearest Point of Relief

The *"nearest point of relief"* is the reference point for taking relief without penalty from interference by an immovable *obstruction* (Rule 24-2), an *abnormal ground condition* (Rule 25-1) or a *wrong putting green* (Rule 25-3).

It is the point on the *course* nearest to where the ball lies, which is not nearer the *hole* and at which, if the ball were so positioned, no interference (as defined) would exist.

**Note:** The player should determine his *nearest point of relief* by using the club with which he expects to play his next *stroke* to simulate the *address* position and swing for such *stroke*.

## Observer

An *"observer"* is one who is appointed by the *Committee* to assist a *referee* to decide questions of fact and to report to him any breach of a *Rule*. An *observer* should not attend the *flagstick*, stand at or mark the position of the *hole*, or lift the ball or mark its position.

## Obstructions

An *"obstruction"* is anything artificial, including the artificial surfaces and sides of roads and paths and manufactured ice, except:

a. Objects defining *out of bounds*, such as walls, fences, stakes and railings;

b. Any part of an immovable artificial object which is *out of bounds;* and

c. Any construction declared by the *Committee* to be an integral part of the *course*.

An *obstruction* is a movable *obstruction* if it may be moved without unreasonable effort, without unduly delaying play and without causing damage. Otherwise it is an immovable *obstruction*.

**Note:** The *Committee* may make a Local Rule declaring a movable *obstruction* to be an immovable *obstruction*.

## Out of Bounds

*"Out of bounds"* is beyond the boundaries of the *course* or any part of the *course* so marked by the *Committee*.

When *out of bounds* is defined by reference to stakes or a fence or as being beyond stakes or a fence, the *out of bounds* line is determined by the nearest inside points of the stakes or fence posts at ground level excluding angled supports.

Objects defining *out of bounds* such as walls, fences, stakes and railings, are not *obstructions* and are deemed to be fixed.

When *out of bounds* is defined by a line on the ground, the line itself is *out of bounds*.

The *out of bounds* line extends vertically upwards and downwards.

A ball is *out of bounds* when all of it lies *out of bounds*.

A player may stand *out of bounds* to play a ball lying within bounds.

## Outside Agency

An *"outside agency"* is any agency not part of the *match* or, in stroke play, not part of the *competitor's side,* and includes a *referee*, a *marker*, an *observer* and a *forecaddie*. Neither wind nor water is an *outside agency*.

## Partner

A *"partner"* is a player associated with another player on the same *side*.

In a threesome, foursome, best-ball or four-ball match, where the context so admits, the word "player" includes his *partner* or *partners*.

## Penalty Stroke

A *"penalty stroke"* is one added to the score of a player or *side* under certain Rules. In a threesome or foursome, *penalty strokes* do not affect the order of play.

## Provisional Ball

A *"provisional ball"* is a ball played under Rule 27-2 for a ball which may be *lost* outside a *water hazard* or may be *out of bounds.*

## Putting Green

The *"putting green"* is all ground of the hole being played which is specially prepared for putting or otherwise defined as such by the *Committee.* A ball is on the *putting green* when any part of it touches the *putting green.*

## Referee

A *"referee"* is one who is appointed by the Committee to accompany players to decide questions of fact and apply the *Rules.* He shall act on any breach of a Rule which he observes or is reported to him.

A *referee* should not attend the *flagstick,* stand at or mark the position of the *hole,* or lift the ball or mark its position.

## Rub of the Green

A *"rub of the green"* occurs when a ball in motion is accidentally deflected or stopped by any *outside agency* (see Rule 19-1).

## Rule

The term "Rule" includes:
a. The Rules of Golf;
b. Any Local Rules made by the *Committee* under Rule 33-8a and Appendix I; and
c. The specifications on clubs and the ball in Appendices II and III.

## Sides and Matches

*Side:* A player, or two or more players who are *partners.*

Single: A match in which one plays against another.

Threesome: A match in which one plays against two, and each *side* plays one ball.

Foursome: A match in which two play against two, and each *side* plays one ball.

Three-Ball: A match play competition in which three play against one another, each playing his own ball. Each player is playing two distinct *matches*.

Best-Ball: A match in which one plays against the better ball of two or the best ball of three players.

Four-Ball: A match in which two play their better ball against the better ball of two other players.

## Stance

Taking the *"stance"* consists in a player placing his feet in position for and preparatory to making a *stroke*.

## Stipulated Round

The *"stipulated round"* consists of playing the holes of the *course* in their correct sequence unless otherwise authorized by the *Committee*. The number of holes in a *stipulated round* is 18 unless a smaller number is authorized by the *Committee*. As to extension of *stipulated round* in match play, see Rule 2-3.

## Stroke

A *"stroke"* is the forward movement of the club made with the intention of fairly striking at and moving the ball, but if a player checks his downswing voluntarily before the clubhead reaches the ball he is deemed not to have made a *stroke*.

## Teeing Ground

The *"teeing ground"* is the starting place for the hole to be played. It is a rectangular area two club-lengths in depth, the front and the sides of which are defined by the outside limits of two tee-markers. A ball is outside the *teeing ground* when all of it lies outside the *teeing ground*.

## Through the Green

"*Through the green*" is the whole area of the *course* except:

a. The *teeing ground* and *putting green* of the hole being played; and

b. All *hazards* on the *course*.

## Water Hazard

A "*water hazard*" is any sea, lake, pond, river, ditch, surface drainage ditch or other open water course (whether or not containing water) and anything of a similar nature.

All ground or water within the margin of a *water hazard* is part of the *water hazard*. The margin of a *water hazard* extends vertically upwards and downwards. Stakes and lines defining the margins of *water hazards* are in the *hazards*. Such stakes are *obstructions*. A ball is in a *water hazard* when it lies in or any part of it touches the *water hazard*.

**Note 1:** *Water hazards* (other than *lateral water hazards*) should be defined by yellow stakes or lines.

**Note 2:** The *Committee* may make a Local Rule prohibiting play from an environmentally-sensitive area which has been defined as a *water hazard*.

## Wrong Ball

A "*wrong ball*" is any ball other than the player's:

a. *Ball in play*,

b. *Provisional ball*, or

  c. Second ball played under Rule 3-3 or Rule 20-7b in
     stroke play.

  *Note: Ball in play* includes a ball substituted for the *ball in play* whether or not such substitution is permitted.

### Wrong Putting Green

  A *"wrong putting green"* is any *putting green* other than that of the hole being played. Unless otherwise prescribed by the *Committee*, this term includes a practice *putting green* or pitching green on the *course*.

# Section III
# *THE RULES OF PLAY*

# The Game

## Rule 1   The Game

### 1-1   General

The Game of Golf consists in playing a ball from the *teeing ground* into the *hole* by a *stroke* or successive *strokes* in accordance with the *Rules*.

### 1-2   Exerting Influence on Ball

No player or *caddie* shall take any action to influence the position or the movement of a ball except in accordance with the *Rules*.

(Removal of movable *obstruction*—see Rule 24-1.)

> PENALTY FOR BREACH OF RULE 1-2:
> Match play—Loss of hole;
> Stroke play—Two strokes.

**Note:** In the case of a serious breach of Rule 1-2, the *Committee* may impose a penalty of disqualification.

### 1-3   Agreement to Waive Rules

Players shall not agree to exclude the operation of any *Rule* or to waive any penalty incurred.

> PENALTY FOR BREACH OF RULE 1-3:
> Match play—Disqualification of both sides;
> Stroke play—Disqualification of
> competitors concerned.

(Agreeing to play out of turn in stroke play—see Rule 10-2c.)

### 1-4   Points Not Covered by Rules

If any point in dispute is not covered by the *Rules*, the decision shall be made in accordance with equity.

---

## Rule 2  Match Play

**2-1  Winner of Hole; Reckoning of Holes**

In match play the game is played by holes.

Except as otherwise provided in the *Rules*, a hole is won by the *side* which *holes* its ball in the fewer *strokes*. In a handicap match the lower net score wins the hole.

The reckoning of holes is kept by the terms: so many "holes up" or "all square," and so many "to play."

A *side* is "dormie" when it is as many holes up as there are holes remaining to be played.

**2-2  Halved Hole**

A hole is halved if each *side holes* out in the same number of *strokes*.

When a player has *holed* out and his opponent has been left with a *stroke* for the half, if the player thereafter incurs a penalty, the hole is halved.

**2-3  Winner of Match**

A match (which consists of a *stipulated round*, unless otherwise decreed by the *Committee*) is won by the *side* which is leading by a number of holes greater than the number of holes remaining to be played.

The *Committee* may, for the purpose of settling a tie, extend the *stipulated round* to as many holes as are required for a match to be won.

**2-4  Concession of Next Stroke, Hole or Match**

When the opponent's ball is at rest or is deemed to be at rest under Rule 16-2, the player may concede the opponent to have *holed* out with his next *stroke* and the ball may be removed by either *side* with a club or otherwise.

A player may concede a hole or a match at any time prior to the conclusion of the hole or the match.

Concession of a *stroke*, hole or match may not be declined or withdrawn.

## 2-5 Claims

In match play, if a doubt or dispute arises between the players and no duly authorized representative of the *Committee* is available within a reasonable time, the players shall continue the match without delay. Any claim, if it is to be considered by the *Committee*, must be made before any player in the match plays from the next *teeing ground* or, in the case of the last hole of the match, before all players in the match leave the *putting green*.

No later claim shall be considered unless it is based on facts previously unknown to the player making the claim and the player making the claim had been given wrong information (Rules 6-2a and 9) by an opponent. In any case, no later claim shall be considered after the result of the match has been officially announced, unless the *Committee* is satisfied that the opponent knew he was giving wrong information.

## 2-6 General Penalty

The penalty for a breach of a *Rule* in match play is loss of hole except when otherwise provided.

## Rule 3    Stroke Play

### 3-1    Winner

The *competitor* who plays the *stipulated round* or rounds in the fewest strokes is the winner.

### 3-2    Failure to Hole Out

If a *competitor* fails to *hole* out at any hole and does not correct his mistake before he plays a *stroke* from the next *teeing ground* or, in the case of the last hole of the round, before he leaves the *putting green*, he shall be disqualified.

### 3-3    Doubt as to Procedure

#### a. Procedure

In stroke play only, when during play of a hole a *competitor* is doubtful of his rights or procedure, he may, without penalty, play a second ball. After the situation which caused the doubt has arisen, the *competitor* should, before taking further action, announce to his *marker* or a *fellow-competitor* his decision to invoke this Rule and the ball with which he will score if the *Rules* permit.

The *competitor* shall report the facts to the *Committee* before returning his score card unless he scores the same with both balls; if he fails to do so, he shall be disqualified.

#### b. Determination of Score for Hole

If the *Rules* allow the procedure selected in advance by the *competitor*, the score with the ball selected shall be his score for the hole.

If the *competitor* fails to announce in advance his decision to invoke this Rule or his selection, the score with the original ball or, if the original ball is not one of the balls being played, the first ball put into play shall count if the *Rules* allow the procedure adopted for such ball.

**Note 1:** If a *competitor* plays a second ball, *penalty strokes* incurred solely by playing the ball ruled not to count and *strokes* subsequently taken with that ball shall be disregarded.

**Note 2:** A second ball played under Rule 3-3 is not a *provisional ball* under Rule 27-2.

### 3-4 Refusal to Comply with a Rule

If a *competitor* refuses to comply with a *Rule* affecting the rights of another *competitor*, he shall be disqualified.

### 3-5 General Penalty

The penalty for a breach of a *Rule* in stroke play is two strokes except when otherwise provided.

# *Clubs and the Ball*

The United States Golf Association reserves the right to change the *Rules* and make and change the interpretations relating to clubs, balls and other implements at any time.

| Rule 4 | Clubs |

A player in doubt as to the conformity of a club should consult the United States Golf Association.

A manufacturer should submit to the United States Golf Association a sample of a club which is to be manufactured for a ruling as to whether the club conforms with the *Rules*. If a manufacturer fails to submit a sample before manufacturing and/or marketing the club, the manufacturer assumes the risk of a ruling that the club does not conform with the *Rules*. Any sample submitted to the United States Golf Association will become its property for reference purposes.

## 4-1 Form and Make of Clubs

### a. General

The player's clubs shall conform with this Rule and the provisions, specifications and inter-pretations set forth in Appendix II.

### b. Wear and Alteration

A club which conforms with the *Rules* when new is deemed to conform after wear through normal use. Any part of a club which has been purposely altered is regarded as new and must, in its altered state, conform with the *Rules*.

## 4-2 Playing Characteristics Changed and Foreign Material

### a. Playing Characteristics Changed

During a *stipulated round*, the playing characteristics of a club shall not be purposely changed by adjustment or by any other means.

### b. Foreign Material

Foreign material must not be applied to the club face for the purpose of influencing the movement of the ball.

> PENALTY FOR BREACH OF RULE 4-1 or -2:
> Disqualification.

## 4-3 Damaged Clubs: Repair and Replacement

### a. Damage in Normal Course of Play

If, during a *stipulated round*, a player's club is damaged in the normal course of play, he may:

(i)   use the club in its damaged state for the remainder of the *stipulated round;* or

(ii)  without unduly delaying play, repair it or have it repaired; or

(iii) as an additional option available only if the club is unfit for play, replace the damaged club with any club. The replacement of a club must not unduly delay play and must not be made by borrowing any club selected for play by any other person playing on the *course.*

> PENALTY FOR BREACH OF RULE 4-3a:
> See Penalty Statement for Rule 4-4a or b.

**Note:** A club is unfit for play if it is substantially damaged, e.g., the shaft breaks into pieces or the clubhead becomes loose, detached or significantly deformed. A club is not unfit for play solely because the shaft is bent, the club's lie or loft has been altered or the clubhead is scratched.

### b. Damage Other Than in Normal Course of Play

If, during a *stipulated round,* a player's club is damaged other than in the normal course of play rendering it non-conforming or changing its playing characteristics, the club shall not subsequently be used or replaced during the round.

### c. Damage Prior to Round

A player may use a club damaged prior to a round provided the club, in its damaged state, conforms with the *Rules.*

Damage to a club which occurred prior to a round may be repaired during the round, provided the playing characteristics are not changed and play is not unduly delayed.

PENALTY FOR BREACH OF RULE 4-3b or c:
Disqualification.

(Undue delay—see Rule 6-7.)

## 4-4 Maximum of Fourteen Clubs

### a. Selection and Addition of Clubs

The player shall start a *stipulated round* with not more than fourteen clubs. He is limited to the clubs thus selected for that round except that, if he started with fewer than fourteen clubs, he may add any number provided his total number does not exceed fourteen.

The addition of a club or clubs must not unduly delay play (Rule 6-7) and must not be made by borrowing any club selected for play by any other person playing on the *course*.

### b. Partners May Share Clubs

*Partners* may share clubs, provided that the total number of clubs carried by the *partners* so sharing does not exceed fourteen.

> PENALTY FOR BREACH OF RULE 4-4a or b,
> REGARDLESS OF NUMBER
> OF EXCESS CLUBS CARRIED:
> Match play—At the conclusion of the hole at which the breach is discovered, the state of the match shall be adjusted by deducting one hole for each hole at which a breach occurred.
> Maximum deduction per round: Two holes.
>
> Stroke play—Two strokes for each hole at which any breach occurred; maximum penalty per round: Four strokes.
>
> Bogey and par competitions—
> Penalties as in match play.
>
> Stableford competitions—see Note to Rule 32-1b.

### c. Excess Club Declared Out of Play

Any club carried or used in breach of this Rule shall be declared out of play by the player immediately upon discovery that a breach has occurred and thereafter shall not be used by the player during the round.

> PENALTY FOR BREACH OF RULE 4-4c:
> Disqualification.

## Rule 5 The Ball

### 5-1 General

The ball the player uses shall conform to requirements specified in Appendix III.

**Note:** The *Committee* may require, in the conditions of a competition (Rule 33-1), that the ball the player uses must be named on the current List of Conforming Golf Balls issued by the United States Golf Association.

### 5-2 Foreign Material

Foreign material must not be applied to a ball for the purpose of changing its playing characteristics.

> PENALTY FOR BREACH OF RULE 5-1 or -2:
> Disqualification.

### 5-3 Ball Unfit for Play

A ball is unfit for play if it is visibly cut, cracked or out of shape. A ball is not unfit for play solely because mud or other materials adhere to it, its surface is scratched or scraped or its paint is damaged or discolored.

If a player has reason to believe his ball has become unfit for play during the play of the *hole* being played, he may during the play of such hole lift his ball without penalty to determine whether it is unfit.

Before lifting the ball, the player must announce his intention to his opponent in match play or his *marker* or a *fellow-competitor* in stroke play and mark the position of the ball. He may then lift and examine the ball without cleaning it and must give his opponent, *marker* or *fellow-competitor* an opportunity to examine the ball.

If he fails to comply with this procedure, he shall incur a penalty of one stroke.

If it is determined that the ball has become unfit for play during play of the hole being played, the player may substitute another ball, placing it on the spot where the original ball lay. Otherwise, the original ball shall be replaced.

If a ball breaks into pieces as a result of a *stroke*, the *stroke* shall be cancelled and the player shall play a ball without penalty as nearly as possible at the spot from which the original ball was played (see Rule 20-5).

> *PENALTY FOR BREACH OF RULE 5-3:
> Match play—Loss of hole;
> Stroke play—Two strokes.
>
> *If a player incurs the general penalty
> for breach of Rule 5-3, no additional penalty
> under the Rule shall be applied.

**Note:** If the opponent, *marker* or *fellow-competitor* wishes to dispute a claim of unfitness, he must do so before the player plays another ball.

(Cleaning ball lifted from *putting green* or under any other Rule—see Rule 21.)

# *Player's Responsibilities*

**Rule 6** The Player

### Definition

A *"marker"* is one who is appointed by the *Committee* to record a *competitor*'s score in stroke play. He may be a *fellow-competitor*. He is not a *referee*.

### 6-1 Rules; Conditions of Competition

The player is responsible for knowing the *Rules* and the conditions under which the competition is to be played (Rule 33-1).

### 6-2 Handicap

#### a. Match Play

Before starting a match in a handicap competition, the players should determine from one another their respective handicaps. If a player begins the match having declared a higher handicap which would affect the number of strokes given or received, he shall be disqualified; otherwise, the player shall play off the declared handicap.

#### b. Stroke Play

In any round of a handicap competition, the *competitor* shall ensure that his handicap is recorded on his score card before it is returned to the *Committee*. If no handicap is recorded on his score card before it is returned, or if the recorded handicap is higher than that to which he is entitled and this affects the number of strokes received, he shall be disqualified from the handicap competition; otherwise, the score shall stand.

**Note:** It is the player's responsibility to know the holes at which handicap strokes are to be given or received.

## 6-3 Time of Starting and Groups

### a. Time of Starting

The player shall start at the time laid down by the *Committee*.

### b. Groups

In stroke play, the *competitor* shall remain throughout the round in the group arranged by the *Committee* unless the *Committee* authorizes or ratifies a change.

> PENALTY FOR BREACH OF RULE 6-3:
> Disqualification.

(Best-ball and four-ball play—see Rules 30-3a and 31-2.)

**Note:** The *Committee* may provide in the conditions of a competition (Rule 33-1) that, if the player arrives at his starting point, ready to play, within five minutes after his starting time, in the absence of circumstances which warrant waiving the penalty of disqualification as provided in Rule 33-7, the penalty for failure to start on time is loss of the first hole in match play or two strokes at the first hole in stroke play instead of disqualification.

### 6-4 Caddie

The player may have only one *caddie* at any one time, under penalty of disqualification.

For any breach of a *Rule* by his *caddie*, the player incurs the applicable penalty.

### 6-5 Ball

The responsibility for playing the proper ball rests with the player. Each player should put an identification mark on his ball.

### 6-6 Scoring in Stroke Play

#### a. Recording Scores

After each hole the *marker* should check the score with the *competitor* and record it. On completion of the round the *marker* shall sign the card and hand it to the *competitor*. If more than one *marker* records the scores, each shall sign for the part for which he is responsible.

#### b. Signing and Returning Card

After completion of the round, the *competitor* should check his score for each hole and settle any doubtful points with the *Committee*. He shall ensure that the *marker* has signed the card, countersign the card himself and return it to the *Committee* as soon as possible.

> PENALTY FOR BREACH OF RULE 6-6b:
> Disqualification.

#### c. Alteration of Card

No alteration may be made on a card after the *competitor* has returned it to the *Committee*.

### d. Wrong Score for Hole

The *competitor* is responsible for the correctness of the score recorded for each hole on his card. If he returns a score for any hole lower than actually taken, he shall be disqualified. If he returns a score for any hole higher than actually taken, the score as returned shall stand.

**Note 1:** The *Committee* is responsible for the addition of scores and application of the handicap recorded on the card—see Rule 33-5.

**Note 2:** In four-ball stroke play, see also Rule 31-4 and -7a.

### 6-7 Undue Delay; Slow Play

The player shall play without undue delay and in accordance with any pace of play guidelines which may be laid down by the *Committee*. Between completion of a hole and playing from the next *teeing ground*, the player shall not unduly delay play.

> PENALTY FOR BREACH OF RULE 6-7:
> Match play—Loss of hole;
> Stroke play—Two strokes.
>
> Bogey and par competitions—
> See Note 2 to Rule 32-1a.
>
> Stableford competitions—
> See Note 2 to Rule 32-1b.
>
> For subsequent offense—Disqualification.

**Note 1:** If the player unduly delays play between holes, he is delaying the play of the next hole and, except for bogey, par and stableford competitions (see Rule 32), the penalty applies to that hole.

**Note 2:** For the purpose of preventing slow play, the *Committee* may, in the conditions of a competition (Rule 33-1), lay down pace of play guidelines including maximum periods of time allowed to complete a *stipulated round*, a hole or a *stroke*.

In stroke play only, the *Committee* may, in such a condition, modify the penalty for a breach of this Rule as follows:

> First offense—One stroke;
> Second offense—Two strokes.
> For subsequent offense—Disqualification.

### 6-8 Discontinuance of Play; Resumption of Play

**a. When Permitted**

The player shall not discontinue play unless:

(i) the *Committee* has suspended play;

(ii) he believes there is danger from lightning;

(iii) he is seeking a decision from the *Committee* on a doubtful or disputed point (see Rules 2-5 and 34-3); or

(iv) there is some other good reason such as sudden illness.

Bad weather is not of itself a good reason for discontinuing play.

If the player discontinues play without specific permission from the *Committee*, he shall report to the *Committee* as soon as practicable. If he does so and the *Committee* considers his reason satisfactory, the player incurs no penalty. Otherwise, the player shall be disqualified.

**Exception in match play:** Players discontinuing match play by agreement are not subject to disqualification unless by so doing the competition is delayed.

*Note:* Leaving the *course* does not of itself constitute discontinuance of play.

### b. Procedure When Play Suspended By Committee

When play is suspended by the *Committee*, if the players in a match or group are between the play of two holes, they shall not resume play until the *Committee* has ordered a resumption of play. If they are in the process of playing a hole, they may continue provided they do so without delay. If they choose to continue, they shall discontinue either before or immediately after completing the hole.

The players shall resume play when the *Committee* has ordered a resumption of play.

> PENALTY FOR BREACH OF RULE 6-8b:
> Disqualification.

**Note:** The *Committee* may provide in the conditions of a competition (Rule 33-1) that, in potentially dangerous situations, play shall be discontinued immediately following a suspension of play by the *Committee*. If a player fails to discontinue play immediately, he shall be disqualified unless circumstances warrant waiving such penalty as provided in Rule 33-7.

### c. Lifting Ball When Play Discontinued

When a player discontinues play of a hole under Rule 6-8a, he may lift his ball without penalty only if the *Committee* has suspended play or there is a good reason to lift it. Before lifting the ball the player must mark its position. If the player discontinues play and lifts his ball without specific permission from the *Committee*, when reporting to the *Committee* (Rule 6-8a), he shall, at that time, report the lifting of the ball.

If the player lifts the ball without a good reason to do so, fails to mark the position of the ball before lifting it or fails to report the lifting of the ball, he shall incur a penalty of one stroke.

### d. Procedure When Play Resumed

Play shall be resumed from where it was discontinued, even if resumption occurs on a subsequent day. The player shall, either before or when play is resumed, proceed as follows:

(i) if the player has lifted the ball, he shall, provided he was entitled to lift it under Rule 6-8c, place a ball on the spot from which the original ball was lifted. Otherwise, the original ball must be replaced;

(ii) if the player entitled to lift his ball under Rule 6-8c has not done so, he may lift, clean and replace the ball, or substitute a ball on the spot from which the original ball was lifted. Before lifting the ball he must mark its position; or

(iii) if the player's ball or ball-marker is moved (including by wind or water) while play is discontinued, a ball or ball-marker shall be placed on the spot from which the original ball or ball-marker was moved. (Spot not determinable—Rule 20-3c.)

> *PENALTY FOR BREACH OF RULE 6-8d:
> Match play—Loss of hole;
>
> Stroke play—Two strokes.
>
> *If a player incurs the general penalty
> for a breach of Rule 6-8d, no additional penalty
> under Rule 6-8c shall be applied.

### Rule 7   Practice

**Definition**

The *"course"* is the whole area within which play is permitted (see Rule 33-2).

### 7-1   Before or Between Rounds

**a.** MATCH PLAY

On any day of a match play competition, a player may practice on the competition *course* before a round.

**b.** STROKE PLAY

On any day of a stroke competition or play-off, a *competitor* shall not practice on the competition *course* or test the surface of any *putting green* on the *course* before a round or play-off. When two or more rounds of a stroke competition are to be played over consecutive days, a competitor shall not practice between those rounds on any competition *course* remaining to be played, or test the surface of any *putting green* on such course.

**Exception:** Practice putting or chipping on or near the first *teeing ground* before starting a round or play-off is permitted.

> PENALTY FOR BREACH OF RULE 7-1b:
> Disqualification.

**Note:** The *Committee* may in the conditions of a competition (Rule 33-1) prohibit practice on the competition *course* on any day of a match play competition or permit practice on the competition *course* or part of the *course* (Rule 33-2c) on any day of or between rounds of a stroke competition.

## 7-2. During Round

A player shall not play a practice *stroke* either during the play of a hole or between the play of two holes except that, between the play of two holes, the player may practice putting or chipping on or near the *putting green* of the hole last played, any practice *putting green* or the *teeing ground* of the next hole to be played in the round, provided such practice *stroke* is not played from a *hazard* and does not unduly delay play (Rule 6-7).

*Strokes* played in continuing the play of a hole, the result of which has been decided, are not practice *strokes*.

**Exception:** When play has been suspended by the *Committee*, a player may, prior to resumption of play, practice (a) as provided in this Rule, (b) anywhere other than on the competition *course* and (c) as otherwise permitted by the *Committee*.

> PENALTY FOR BREACH OF RULE 7-2:
> Match play—Loss of hole;
> Stroke play—Two strokes.
>
> In the event of a breach between the play of two holes, the penalty applies to the next hole.

Note 1: A practice swing is not a practice *stroke* and may be taken at any place, provided the player does not breach the *Rules*.

Note 2: The *Committee* may prohibit practice on or near the *putting green* of the hole last played.

## Rule 8    Advice; Indicating Line of Play

### Definitions

*"Advice"* is any counsel or suggestion which could influence a player in determining his play, the choice of a club or the method of making a *stroke*.

Information on the *Rules* or on matters of public information, such as the position of *hazards* or the *flagstick* on the *putting green*, is not *advice*.

The *"line of play"* is the direction which the player wishes his ball to take after a *stroke*, plus a reasonable distance on either side of the intended direction. The *line of play* extends vertically upwards from the ground, but does not extend beyond the *hole*.

### 8-1   Advice

During a *stipulated round*, a player shall not give *advice* to anyone in the competition except his *partner* and may ask for *advice* only from his *partner* or either of their *caddies*.

### 8-2   Indicating Line of Play

#### a. Other Than on Putting Green

Except on the *putting green,* a player may have the *line of play* indicated to him by anyone, but no one shall be positioned by the player on or close to the line or an extension of the line

beyond the *hole* while the *stroke* is being played.
Any mark placed during the play of a hole by
the player or with his knowledge to indicate the
line shall be removed before the *stroke* is played.

**Exception:** *Flagstick* attended or held up—see
Rule 17-1.

### b. On the Putting Green

When the player's ball is on the *putting green,*
the player, his *partner* or either of their *caddies*
may, before but not during the *stroke,* point out
a line for putting, but in so doing the *putting
green* shall not be touched. No mark shall be
placed anywhere to indicate a line for putting.

> PENALTY FOR BREACH OF RULE:
> Match play—Loss of hole;
> Stroke play—Two strokes.

**Note:** The *Committee* may, in the conditions of
a team competition (Rule 33-1), permit each team
to appoint one person who may give *advice*
(including pointing out a line for putting) to
members of that team. The *Committee* may lay
down conditions relating to the appointment and
permitted conduct of such person, who must be
identified to the *Committee* before giving *advice.*

## Rule 9   Information as to Strokes Taken

### 9-1   General

The number of *strokes* a player has taken shall
include any *penalty strokes* incurred.

## 9-2 Match Play

A player who has incurred a penalty shall inform his opponent as soon as practicable, unless he is obviously proceeding under a *Rule* involving a penalty and this has been observed by his opponent. If he fails so to inform his opponent, he shall be deemed to have given wrong information, even if he was not aware that he had incurred a penalty.

An opponent is entitled to ascertain from the player, during the play of a hole, the number of *strokes* he has taken and, after play of a hole, the number of *strokes* taken on the hole just completed.

If during the play of a hole the player gives or is deemed to give wrong information as to the number of *strokes* taken, he shall incur no penalty if he corrects the mistake before his opponent has played his next *stroke*. If the player fails so to correct the wrong information, he shall lose the hole.

If after play of a hole the player gives or is deemed to give wrong information as to the number of *strokes* taken on the hole just completed and this affects the opponent's understanding of the result of the hole, he shall incur no penalty if he corrects his mistake before any player plays from the next *teeing ground* or, in the case of the last hole of the match, before all players leave the *putting green*. If the player fails so to correct the wrong information, he shall lose the hole.

## 9-3 Stroke Play

A *competitor* who has incurred a penalty should inform his *marker* as soon as practicable.

# *Order of Play*

## Rule 10   Order of Play

### Definition

The player who is to play first from the *teeing ground* is said to have the *"honor."*

### 10-1   Match Play

#### a. Teeing Ground

The *side* which shall have the *honor* at the first *teeing ground* shall be determined by the order of the draw. In the absence of a draw, the *honor* should be decided by lot.

The *side* which wins a hole shall take the *honor* at the next *teeing ground*. If a hole has been halved, the *side* which had the *honor* at the previous *teeing ground* shall retain it.

#### b. Other Than on Teeing Ground

When the *balls are in play*, the ball farther from the *hole* shall be played first. If the balls are equidistant from the *hole*, the ball to be played first should be decided by lot.

**Exception:** Rule 30-3c (best-ball and four-ball match play).

#### c. Playing Out of Turn

If a player plays when his opponent should have played, the opponent may immediately require the player to cancel the *stroke* so played and, in correct order, play a ball without penalty as nearly as possible at the spot from which the original ball was last played (see Rule 20-5).

## 10-2 Stroke Play

### a. Teeing Ground

The *competitor* who shall have the *honor* at the first *teeing ground* shall be determined by the order of the draw. In the absence of a draw, the *honor* should be decided by lot.

The *competitor* with the lowest score at a *hole* shall take the *honor* at the next *teeing ground*. The *competitor* with the second lowest score shall play next and so on. If two or more *competitors* have the same score at a hole, they shall play from the next *teeing ground* in the same order as at the previous *teeing ground*.

### b. Other Than on Teeing Ground

When the *balls are in play,* the ball farthest from the *hole* shall be played first. If two or more balls are equidistant from the *hole*, the ball to be played first should be decided by lot.

**Exceptions:** Rules 22 (ball interfering with or assisting play) and 31-5 (four-ball stroke play).

### c. Playing Out of Turn

If a *competitor* plays out of turn, no penalty is incurred and the ball shall be played as it lies. If, however, the *Committee* determines that *competitors* have agreed to play in an order other than that set forth in Clauses 2a, 2b and 3 of this Rule to give one of them an advantage, they shall be disqualified.

(Incorrect order of play in threesomes and foursomes stroke play—see Rule 29-3.)

(Playing stroke while another ball in motion

after stroke from putting green—see Rule 16-1f.)

## 10-3 Provisional Ball or Second Ball from Teeing Ground

If a player plays a *provisional ball* or a second ball from a *teeing ground,* he shall do so after his opponent or *fellow-competitor* has played his first *stroke.* If a player plays a *provisional ball* or a second ball out of turn, Clauses 1c and 2c of this Rule shall apply.

## 10-4 Ball Moved in Measuring

If a ball is *moved* in measuring to determine which ball is farther from the *hole,* no penalty is incurred and the ball shall be replaced.

# *Teeing Ground*

### Rule 11    Teeing Ground

**Definition**

The *"teeing ground"* is the starting place for the hole to be played. It is a rectangular area two club-lengths in depth, the front and the sides of which are defined by the outside limits of two tee-markers. A ball is outside the *teeing ground* when all of it lies outside the *teeing ground.*

## 11-1 Teeing

In teeing, the ball may be placed on the ground, on an irregularity of surface created by the player on the ground or on a tee, sand or other substance in order to raise it off the ground.

A player may stand outside the *teeing ground* to play a ball within it.

## 11-2 Tee-Markers

Before a player plays his first *stroke* with any ball from the *teeing ground* of the hole being played, the tee-markers are deemed to be fixed. In such circumstances, if the player moves or allows to be moved a tee-marker for the purpose of avoiding interference with his *stance*, the area of his intended swing or his *line of play*, he shall incur the penalty for a breach of Rule 13-2.

## 11-3 Ball Falling Off Tee

If a ball, when not in play, falls off a tee or is knocked off a tee by the player in *addressing* it, it may be re-teed without penalty, but if a *stroke* is made at the ball in these circumstances, whether the ball is moving or not, the *stroke* counts but no penalty is incurred.

## 11-4 Playing from Outside Teeing Ground

### a. Match Play

If a player, when starting a hole, plays a ball from outside the *teeing ground*, the opponent may immediately require the player to cancel the *stroke* so played and play a ball from within the *teeing ground*, without penalty.

### b. Stroke Play

If a *competitor*, when starting a hole, plays a ball from outside the *teeing ground*, he shall incur a penalty of two strokes and shall then play a ball from within the *teeing ground*.

If the *competitor* plays a *stroke* from the next *teeing ground* without first correcting his mistake or, in the case of the last hole of the round, leaves the *putting green* without first declaring his intention to correct his mistake, he shall be disqualified.

The *stroke* from outside the *teeing ground* and any subsequent *strokes* by the *competitor* on the hole prior to his correction of the mistake do not count in his score.

## 11-5 Playing from Wrong Teeing Ground

The provisions of Rule 11-4 apply.

# *Playing the Ball*

### Rule 12   Searching for and Identifying Ball

#### Definitions

A *"hazard"* is any *bunker* or *water hazard*.

A *"bunker"* is a *hazard* consisting of a prepared area of ground, often a hollow, from which turf or soil has been removed and replaced with sand or the like. Grass-covered ground bordering or within a *bunker* is not part of the *bunker*. The margin of a *bunker* extends vertically downwards, but not upwards. A ball is in a *bunker* when it lies in or any part of it touches the *bunker*.

A *"water hazard"* is any sea, lake, pond, river, ditch, surface drainage ditch or other open water course (whether or not containing water) and anything of a similar nature.

All ground or water within the margin of a *water hazard* is part of the *water hazard*. The margin of a *water hazard* extends vertically upwards and downwards. Stakes and lines defining the margins of *water hazards* are in the *hazards*. Such stakes are *obstructions*. A ball is in a *water hazard* when it lies in or any part of it touches the *water hazard*.

**Note 1:** *Water hazards* (other than *lateral water hazards*) should be defined by yellow stakes or lines.

**Note 2:** The *Committee* may make a Local Rule prohibiting play from an environmentally-sensitive area which has been defined as a *water hazard*.

**12-1 Searching for Ball; Seeing Ball**

In searching for his ball anywhere on the *course*, the player may touch or bend long grass, rushes, bushes, whins, heather or the like, but only to the extent necessary to find and identify it, provided that this does not improve the lie of the ball, the area of his intended swing or his *line of play*.

A player is not necessarily entitled to see his ball when playing a *stroke*.

In a *hazard*, if a ball is believed to be covered by *loose impediments* or sand, the player may remove by probing, raking or other means as much thereof as will enable him to see a part of the ball. If an excess is removed, no penalty is incurred and the ball shall be re-covered so that only a part of the ball is visible. If the ball is *moved* in such removal, no penalty is incurred; the ball shall be replaced and, if necessary, re-covered. As to removal of *loose impediments* outside a *hazard*, see Rule 23.

If a ball lying in an *abnormal ground condition* is accidentally *moved* during search, no penalty is incurred; the ball shall be replaced, unless the player elects to proceed under Rule 25-1b. If the player replaces the ball, he may still proceed under

Rule 25-1b if applicable.

If a ball is believed to be lying in water in a *water hazard,* the player may probe for it with a club or otherwise. If the ball is *moved* in so doing, no penalty is incurred; the ball shall be replaced, unless the player elects to proceed under Rule 26-1.

> PENALTY FOR BREACH OF RULE 12-1:
> Match play—Loss of hole;
> Stroke play—Two strokes.

## 12-2 Identifying Ball

The responsibility for playing the proper ball rests with the player. Each player should put an identification mark on his ball.

Except in a *hazard,* the player may, without penalty, lift a ball he believes to be his own for the purpose of identification and clean it to the extent necessary for identification. If the ball is the player's ball, he shall replace it. Before lifting the ball, the player must announce his intention to his opponent in match play or his *marker* or a *fellow-competitor* in stroke play and mark the position of the ball. He must then give his opponent, *marker* or *fellow-competitor* an opportunity to observe the lifting and replacement. If he lifts his ball without announcing his intention in advance, marking the position of the ball or giving his opponent, *marker* or *fellow-competitor* an opportunity to observe, or if he lifts his ball for identification in a *hazard,* or cleans it more than necessary for identification, he shall incur a penalty of one stroke and the ball shall be replaced.

If a player who is required to replace a ball fails to do so, he shall incur the penalty for a breach of Rule 20-3a, but no additional penalty under Rule 12-2 shall be applied.

## Rule 13    Ball Played as It Lies

### Definitions

A *"hazard"* is any *bunker* or *water hazard.*

A *"bunker"* is a *hazard* consisting of a prepared area of ground, often a hollow, from which turf or soil has been removed and replaced with sand or the like. Grass-covered ground bordering or within a *bunker* is not part of the *bunker.* The margin of a *bunker* extends vertically downwards, but not upwards. A ball is in a *bunker* when it lies in or any part of it touches the *bunker.*

A *"water hazard"* is any sea, lake, pond, river, ditch, surface drainage ditch or other open water course (whether or not containing water) and anything of a similar nature.

All ground or water within the margin of a *water hazard* is part of the *water hazard.* The margin of a *water hazard* extends vertically upwards and downwards. Stakes and lines defining the margins of *water hazards* are in the *hazards.* Such stakes are *obstructions.* A ball is in a *water hazard* when it lies in or any part of it touches the *water hazard.*

The *"line of play"* is the direction which the player wishes his ball to take after a *stroke*, plus a reasonable distance on either side of the intended direction. The *line of play* extends vertically upwards from the ground, but does not extend beyond the *hole*.

Taking the *"stance"* consists in a player placing his feet in position for and preparatory to making a *stroke*.

### 13-1 General

The ball shall be played as it lies, except as otherwise provided in the *Rules*.

(Ball at rest *moved*—see Rule 18.)

### 13-2 Improving Lie, Area of Intended Stance or Swing, or Line of Play

Except as provided in the *Rules*, a player shall not improve or allow to be improved:

- the position or lie of his ball,
- the area of his intended *stance* or swing,
- his *line of play* or a reasonable extension of that line beyond the *hole,* or
- the area in which he is to drop or place a ball

by any of the following actions:

- moving, bending or breaking anything growing or fixed (including immovable *obstructions* and objects defining *out of bounds*), creating or eliminating irregularities of surface,
- removing or pressing down sand, loose soil, replaced divots or other cut turf placed in position, or
- removing dew, frost or water

except as follows:

- as may occur in fairly taking his *stance,*

- in making a *stroke* or the backward movement of his club for a *stroke*,
- on the *teeing ground* in creating or eliminating irregularities of surface, or
- on the *putting green* in removing sand and loose soil as provided in Rule 16-1a or in repairing damage as provided in Rule 16-1c.

The club may be grounded only lightly and shall not be pressed on the ground.

**Exception:** Ball in *hazard*—see Rule 13-4.

## 13-3  Building Stance

A player is entitled to place his feet firmly in taking his *stance*, but he shall not build a *stance*.

## 13-4  Ball in Hazard

Except as provided in the *Rules*, before making a *stroke* at a ball which is in a *hazard* (whether a *bunker* or a *water hazard*) or which, having been lifted from a *hazard*, may be dropped or placed in the *hazard*, the player shall not:

a. Test the condition of the *hazard* or any similar *hazard*,

b. Touch the ground in the *hazard* or water in the *water hazard* with a club or otherwise, or

c. Touch or move a *loose impediment* lying in or touching the *hazard*.

### Exceptions:
1.  Provided nothing is done which constitutes testing the condition of the *hazard* or improves the lie of the ball, there is no penalty if the player (a) touches the

ground in any *hazard* or water in a *water hazard* as a result of or to prevent falling, in removing an *obstruction*, in measuring or in retrieving, lifting, placing or replacing a ball under any *Rule* or (b) places his clubs in a *hazard*.

2. The player after playing the *stroke*, or his *caddie* at any time without the authority of the player, may smooth sand or soil in the *hazard*, provided that, if the ball is still in the *hazard*, nothing is done which improves the lie of the ball or assists the player in his subsequent play of the hole.

**Note:** At any time, including at *address* or in the backward movement for the *stroke*, the player may touch with a club or otherwise any *obstruction*, any construction declared by the *Committee* to be an integral part of the *course* or any grass, bush, tree or other growing thing.

> PENALTY FOR BREACH OF RULE:
> Match play—Loss of hole
> Stroke play—Two strokes.

(Searching for ball—see Rule 12-1.)

### Rule 14 Striking the Ball

#### Definition

A *"stroke"* is the forward movement of the club made with the intention of fairly striking at and moving the ball, but if a player checks his downswing voluntarily before the clubhead reaches the ball he is deemed not to have made a *stroke*.

14-1  **Ball to Be Fairly Struck At**

The ball shall be fairly struck at with the head of the club and must not be pushed, scraped or spooned.

14-2  **Assistance**

In making a *stroke*, a player shall not:

a. Accept physical assistance or protection from the elements, or

b. Allow his *caddie*, his *partner* or his *partner's caddie* to position himself on or close to an extension of the *line of play* or the *line of putt* behind the ball.

> PENALTY FOR BREACH OF RULE 14-1 or -2:
> Match play—Loss of hole
> Stroke play—Two strokes.

14-3  **Artificial Devices and Unusual Equipment**

A player in doubt as to whether use of an item would constitute a breach of Rule 14-3 should consult the United States Golf Association.

A manufacturer may submit to the United States Golf Association a sample of an item which is to be manufactured for a ruling as to whether its use during a *stipulated round* would cause a player to be in breach of Rule 14-3. Such sample will become the property of the United States Golf Association for reference purposes. If a manufacturer fails to submit a sample before manufacturing and/or marketing the item, the manufacturer assumes the risk of a ruling that use of the item would be contrary to the Rules of Golf.

Except as provided in the *Rules*, during a *stipulated round* the player shall not use any artificial device or unusual *equipment*:

a. Which might assist him in making a *stroke* or in his play; or

b. For the purpose of gauging or measuring distance or conditions which might affect his play; or

c. Which might assist him in gripping the club, except that:
   - (i)   plain gloves may be worn;
   - (ii)  resin, powder and drying or moisturizing agents may be used; and
   - (iii) a towel or handkerchief may be wrapped around the grip.

PENALTY FOR BREACH OF RULE 14-3:
Disqualification.

### 14-4  Striking the Ball More than Once

If a player's club strikes the ball more than once in the course of a *stroke*, the player shall count the *stroke* and add a penalty stroke, making two strokes in all.

### 14-5  Playing Moving Ball

A player shall not play while his ball is moving.

**Exceptions:**

Ball falling off tee—Rule 11-3.

Striking the ball more than once—Rule 14-4.

Ball moving in water—Rule 14-6.

When the ball begins to *move* only after the player has begun the *stroke* or the backward movement of his club for the *stroke*, he shall incur no penalty under this Rule for playing a moving ball, but he is not exempt from any penalty incurred under the following Rules:

> Ball at rest *moved* by player—Rule 18-2a.
>
> Ball at rest moving after *address*—Rule 18-2b.
>
> Ball at rest moving after *loose impediment* touched—Rule 18-2c.
>
> Ball purposely deflected or stopped by player, *partner* or *caddie*—see Rule 1-2.)

### 14-6 Ball Moving in Water

When a ball is moving in water in a *water hazard*, the player may, without penalty, make a *stroke*, but he must not delay making his *stroke* in order to allow the wind or current to improve the position of the ball. A ball moving in water in a *water hazard* may be lifted if the player elects to invoke Rule 26.

> PENALTY FOR BREACH OF RULE 14-5 or -6:
> Match play—Loss of hole;
> Stroke play;—Two strokes.

### Rule 15 Wrong Ball; Substituted Ball

**Definition**

A *"wrong ball"* is any ball other than the player's:

a. *Ball in play*,

b. *Provisional ball* or

c. Second ball played under Rule 3-3 or Rule 20-7b in stroke play.

**Note:** *Ball in play* includes a ball substituted for the *ball in play*, whether or not such substitution is permitted.

## 15-1 General

A player must hole out with the ball played from the *teeing ground* unless a *Rule* permits him to substitute another ball. If a player substitutes another ball when not so permitted, that ball is not a *wrong ball*; it becomes the *ball in play* and, if the error is not corrected as provided in Rule 20-6, the player shall incur a penalty of loss of hole in match play or two strokes in stroke play.

(Playing from wrong place—see Rule 20-7.)

## 15-2 Match Play

If a player plays a *stroke* with a *wrong ball* except in a *hazard*, he shall lose the hole.

If a player plays any *strokes* in a *hazard* with a *wrong ball*, there is no penalty. *Strokes* played in a *hazard* with a *wrong ball* do not count in the player's score. If the *wrong ball* belongs to another player, its owner shall place a ball on the spot from which the *wrong ball* was first played.

If the player and opponent exchange balls during the play of a hole, the first to play the *wrong ball* other than from a *hazard* shall lose the hole; when this cannot be determined, the hole shall be played out with the balls exchanged.

## 15-3 Stroke Play

If a *competitor* plays a *stroke* or *strokes* with a *wrong ball*, he shall incur a penalty of two strokes, unless the only *stroke* or *strokes* played with such ball were played when it was in a *hazard*, in which case no penalty is incurred.

The *competitor* must correct his mistake by playing the correct ball. If he fails to correct his mistake before he plays a *stroke* from the next *teeing ground* or, in the case of the last hole of the round, fails to declare his intention to correct his mistake before leaving the *putting green*, he shall be disqualified.

*Strokes* played by a *competitor* with a *wrong ball* do not count in his score.

If the *wrong ball* belongs to another *competitor*, its owner shall place a ball on the spot from which the *wrong ball* was first played.

(Lie of ball to be placed or replaced altered—see Rule 20-3b.)

## *The Putting Green*

**Rule 16**   **The Putting Green**

**Definitions**

The *"putting green"* is all ground of the hole being played which is specially prepared for putting or otherwise defined as such by the *Committee*. A ball is on the *putting green* when any part of it touches the *putting green*.

The *"line of putt"* is the line which the player wishes his ball to take after a *stroke* on the *putting green*. Except with respect to Rule 16-1e, the *line of putt* includes a reasonable distance on either side of the intended line. The *line of putt* does not extend beyond the *hole*.

A ball is *"holed"* when it is at rest within the

circumference of the *hole* and all of it is below the level of the lip of the *hole*.

## 16-1 General

### a. Touching Line of Putt

The *line of putt* must not be touched except:

(i) the player may move sand and loose soil on the *putting green* and other *loose impediments* by picking them up or by brushing them aside with his hand or a club without pressing anything down;

(ii) in *addressing the ball*, the player may place the club in front of the ball without pressing anything down;

(iii) in measuring—Rule 10-4;

(iv) in lifting the ball—Rule 16-1b;

(v) in pressing down a ball-marker;

(vi) in repairing old *hole* plugs or ball marks on the *putting green*—Rule 16-1c; and

(vii) in removing movable *obstructions*—Rule 24-1.

(Indicating line for putting on *putting green*—see Rule 8-2b.)

### b. Lifting Ball

A ball on the *putting green* may be lifted and, if desired, cleaned. A ball so lifted shall be replaced on the spot from which it was lifted.

### c. Repair of Hole Plugs, Ball Marks and Other Damage

The player may repair an old *hole* plug or damage to the *putting green* caused by the impact of a ball, whether or not the player's ball lies on the *putting green.* If a ball or ball-marker is accidentally *moved* in the process of such repair, the ball or ball-marker shall be replaced, without penalty. Any other damage to the *putting green* shall not be repaired if it might assist the player in his subsequent play of the hole.

### d. Testing Surface

During the play of a hole, a player shall not test the surface of the *putting green* by rolling a ball or roughening or scraping the surface.

### e. Standing Astride or on Line of Putt

The player shall not make a *stroke* on the *putting green* from a *stance* astride, or with either foot touching, the *line of putt* or an extension of that line behind the ball.

### f. Playing Stroke While Another Ball in Motion

The player shall not play a *stroke* while another ball is in motion after a *stroke* from the *putting green,* except that, if a player does so, he incurs no penalty if it was his turn to play.

(Lifting ball interfering with or assisting play while another ball in motion—see Rule 22.)

> PENALTY FOR BREACH OF RULE 16-1:
> Match play —Loss of hole;
> Stroke play—Two strokes.

(Position of *caddie* or *partner*—see Rule 14-2.)
(*Wrong putting green*—see Rule 25-3)

16-2.    **Ball Overhanging Hole**

When any part of the ball overhangs the lip of
the *hole*, the player is allowed enough time to reach
the *hole* without unreasonable delay and an additional ten seconds to determine whether the ball is
at rest. If by then the ball has not fallen into the
*hole*, it is deemed to be at rest. If the ball subsequently falls into the *hole*, the player is deemed to
have *holed* out with his last *stroke*, and he shall add
a *penalty stroke* to his score for the hole; otherwise
there is no penalty under this Rule.

(Undue delay—see Rule 6-7.)

## Rule 17    The Flagstick

**Definition**

The *"flagstick"* is a movable straight indicator,
with or without bunting or other material
attached, centered in the *hole* to show its position.
It shall be circular in cross-section.

17-1    **Flagstick Attended, Removed or Held Up**

Before and during the *stroke*, the player may
have the *flagstick* attended, removed or held up to
indicate the position of the *hole*. This may be done
only on the authority of the player before he plays
his *stroke*.

If, prior to the *stroke*, the *flagstick* is attended,
removed or held up by anyone with the player's
knowledge and no objection is made, the player
shall be deemed to have authorized it. If anyone
attends or holds up the *flagstick* or stands near the
*hole* while a *stroke* is being played, he shall be

deemed to be attending the *flagstick* until the ball comes to rest.

### 17-2 Unauthorized Attendance

#### a. Match Play

In match play, an opponent or his *caddie* shall not, without the authority or prior knowledge of the player, attend, remove or hold up the *flagstick* while the player is making a *stroke* or his ball is in motion.

#### b. Stroke Play

In stroke play, if a *fellow-competitor* or his *caddie* attends, removes or holds up the *flagstick* without the *competitor*'s authority or prior knowledge while the *competitor* is making a *stroke* or his ball is in motion, the *fellow-competitor* shall incur the penalty for breach of this Rule. In such circumstances, if the *competitor*'s ball strikes the *flagstick*, the person attending it or anything carried by him, the *competitor* incurs no penalty and the ball shall be played as it lies, except that, if the *stroke* was played from the *putting green*, the *stroke* shall be cancelled, the ball replaced and the *stroke* replayed.

> PENALTY FOR BREACH OF RULE 17-1 or -2:
> Match play—Loss of hole;
> Stroke play—Two strokes.

### 17-3 Ball Striking Flagstick or Attendant

The player's ball shall not strike:

a. The *flagstick* when attended, removed or held up by the player, his *partner* or either of their *caddies*, or by another person with the player's authority or prior knowledge; or

b. The player's *caddie*, his *partner* or his *partner's caddie* when attending the *flagstick*, or another person attending the *flagstick* with the player's authority or prior knowledge or anything carried by any such person; or

c. The *flagstick* in the *hole*, unattended, when the ball has been played from the *putting green*.

> PENALTY FOR BREACH OF RULE 17-3:
> Match play—Loss of hole;
> Stroke play —Two strokes
> and the ball shall be played as it lies.

**17-4  Ball Resting Against Flagstick**

If the ball rests against the *flagstick* when it is in the *hole*, the player or another person authorized by him may move or remove the *flagstick* and if the ball falls into the *hole*, the player shall be deemed to have *holed* out with his last *stroke*; otherwise, the ball, if *moved*, shall be placed on the lip of the *hole*, without penalty.

## *Ball Moved, Deflected or Stopped*

**Rule 18**   Ball at Rest Moved

### Definitions

A ball is deemed to have *"moved"* if it leaves its position and comes to rest in any other place.

An *"outside agency"* is any agency not part of the match or, in stroke play, not part of the *competitor's side*, and includes a *referee*, a *marker*, an *observer* and a *forecaddie*. Neither wind nor water is an *outside agency.*

*"Equipment"* is anything used, worn or carried by or for the player except any ball he has played at the hole being played and any small object, such as a coin or a tee, when used to mark the position of a ball or the extent of an area in which a ball is to be dropped. *Equipment* includes a golf cart, whether or not motorized. If such a cart is shared by two or more players, the cart and everything in it are deemed to be the *equipment* of the player whose ball is involved except that, when the cart is being *moved* by one of the players sharing it, the cart and everything in it are deemed to be that player's *equipment.*

**Note:** A ball played at the hole being played is *equipment* when it has been lifted and not put back into play.

A player has *"addressed the ball"* when he has taken his *stance* and has also grounded his club, except that in a *hazard* a player has *addressed the ball* when he has taken his *stance.*

Taking the *"stance"* consists in a player placing

his feet in position for and preparatory to making a *stroke*.

## 18-1 By Outside Agency

If a ball at rest is *moved* by an *outside agency,* the player shall incur no penalty and the ball shall be replaced before the player plays another *stroke*.

(Player's ball at rest *moved* by another ball—see Rule 18-5.)

## 18-2 By Player, Partner, Caddie or Equipment

### a. General

When a player's *ball is in play*, if:

(i) the player, his *partner* or either of their *caddies* lifts or *moves* it, touches it purposely (except with a club in the act of *addressing* it) or causes it to *move* except as permitted by a *Rule*, or

(ii) *equipment* of the player or his *partner* causes the ball to move,

the player shall incur a *penalty stroke.*

The ball shall be replaced unless the movement of the ball occurs after the player has begun his swing and he does not discontinue his swing.

Under the *Rules* no penalty is incurred if a player accidentally causes his ball to *move* in the following circumstances:

In measuring to determine which ball farther from *hole*—Rule 10-4

In searching for covered ball in *hazard* or for ball in *abnormal ground condition*—Rule 12-1

In the process of repairing *hole* plug or ball mark—Rule 16-1c

In the process of removing *loose impediment* on *putting green*—Rule 18-2c

In the process of lifting ball under a *Rule*— Rule 20-1

In the process of placing or replacing ball under a *Rule*—Rule 20-3a

In removal of movable *obstruction*— Rule 24-1.

#### b. Ball Moving After Address

If a player's *ball in play moves* after he has *addressed* it (other than as a result of a *stroke*), the player shall be deemed to have *moved* the ball and shall incur a *penalty stroke.* The player shall replace the ball unless the movement of the ball occurs after he has begun his swing and he does not discontinue his swing.

#### c. Ball Moving After Loose Impediment Touched

*Through the green*, if the ball *moves* after any *loose impediment* lying within a club-length of it has been touched by the player, his *partner* or either of their *caddies* and before the player has *addressed it*, the player shall be deemed to have *moved* the ball and shall incur a *penalty stroke.* The player shall replace the ball unless the movement of the ball occurs after he has begun his swing and he does not discontinue his swing.

On the *putting green*, if the ball or the ball-marker *moves* in the process of removing any *loose*

---

*impediment,* the ball or the ball-marker shall be replaced. There is no penalty provided the movement of the ball or the ball-marker is directly attributable to the removal of the *loose impediment.* Otherwise, the player shall incur a *penalty stroke* under Rule 18-2a or 20-1.

### 18-3 By Opponent, Caddie or Equipment in Match Play

#### a. During Search

If, during search for a player's ball, the ball is *moved* by an opponent, his *caddie* or his *equipment,* no penalty is incurred and the player shall replace the ball.

#### b. Other Than During Search

If, other than during search for a ball, the ball is touched or *moved* by an opponent, his *caddie* or his *equipment,* except as otherwise provided in the Rules, the opponent shall incur a *penalty stroke.* The player shall replace the ball.

(Ball *moved* in measuring to determine which ball farther from the *hole*—see Rule 10-4.)

(Playing a *wrong ball*—see Rule 15-2.)

### 18-4 By Fellow-Competitor, Caddie or Equipment in Stroke Play

If a *competitor*'s ball is *moved* by a *fellow-competitor,* his *caddie* or his *equipment,* no penalty is incurred. The *competitor* shall replace his ball.

(Playing a *wrong ball*—see Rule 15-3.)

18-5 **By Another Ball**

If a *ball in play* and at rest is *moved* by another ball in motion after a *stroke*, the *moved* ball shall be replaced.

> **\*PENALTY FOR BREACH OF RULE:**
> Match play—Loss of hole;
> Stroke play—Two strokes.
>
> *If a player who is required to replace a ball fails to do so, he shall incur the general penalty for breach of Rule 18 but no additional penalty under Rule 18 shall be applied.

**Note 1:** If a ball to be replaced under this Rule is not immediately recoverable, another ball may be substituted.

**Note 2:** If it is impossible to determine the spot on which a ball is to be placed, see Rule 20-3c.

Rule 19 **Ball in Motion Deflected or Stopped**

**Definitions**

An *"outside agency"* is any agency not part of the match or, in stroke play, not part of the *competitor*'s *side*, and includes a *referee*, a *marker*, an *observer* and a *forecaddie*. Neither wind nor water is an *outside agency*.

*"Equipment"* is anything used, worn or carried by or for the player except any ball he has played at the hole being played and any small object, such as a coin or a tee, when used to mark the position of a ball or the extent of an area in which a ball is to be dropped. *Equipment* includes a golf cart, whether or not motorized. If such a cart is shared

by two or more players, the cart and everything in it are deemed to be the *equipment* of the player whose ball is involved except that, when the cart is being moved by one of the players sharing it, the cart and everything in it are deemed to be that player's *equipment*.

**Note:** A ball played at the hole being played is *equipment* when it has been lifted and not put back into play.

### 19-1 By Outside Agency

If a ball in motion is accidentally deflected or stopped by any *outside agency,* it is a *rub of the green*, no penalty is incurred and the ball shall be played as it lies except:

a. If a ball in motion after a *stroke* other than on the *putting green* comes to rest in or on any moving or animate *outside agency,* the player shall, *through the green* or in a *hazard*, drop the ball, or on the *putting green* place the ball, as near as possible to the spot where the *outside agency* was when the ball came to rest in or on it, and

b. If a ball in motion after a *stroke* on the *putting green* is deflected or stopped by, or comes to rest in or on, any moving or animate *outside agency* except a worm or an insect, the *stroke* shall be cancelled, the ball replaced and the *stroke* replayed.

If the ball is not immediately recoverable, another ball may be substituted.

(Player's ball deflected or stopped by another ball—see Rule 19-5.)

**Note:** If the *referee* or the *Committee* determines

that a player's ball has been purposely deflected or stopped by an *outside agency,* Rule 1-4 applies to the player. If the *outside agency* is a *fellow-competitor* or his *caddie,* Rule 1-2 applies to the *fellow-competitor.*

### 19-2 By Player, Partner, Caddie or Equipment

#### a. Match Play

If a player's ball is accidentally deflected or stopped by himself, his *partner* or either of their *caddies* or *equipment,* he shall lose the hole.

#### b. Stroke Play

If a *competitor*'s ball is accidentally deflected or stopped by himself, his *partner* or either of their *caddies* or *equipment,* the *competitor* shall incur a penalty of two strokes. The ball shall be played as it lies, except when it comes to rest in or on the *competitor*'s, his *partner*'s or either of their *caddies*' clothes or *equipment,* in which case the *competitor* shall through the green or in a *hazard* drop the ball, or on the *putting green* place the ball, as near as possible to where the article was when the ball came to rest in or on it.

**Exception:** Dropped ball—see Rule 20-2a.

(Ball purposely deflected or stopped by player, *partner* or *caddie*—see Rule 1-2.)

### 19-3 By Opponent, Caddie or Equipment in Match Play

If a player's ball is accidentally deflected or stopped by an opponent, his *caddie* or his *equipment,* no penalty is incurred. The player may play the ball as it lies or, before another *stroke* is played by either *side,* cancel the *stroke* and play a ball without penalty as nearly as possible at the spot from which the original ball was last played (see Rule 20-5).

If the ball has come to rest in or on the opponent's or his *caddie's* clothes or *equipment,* the player may *through the green* or in a *hazard* drop the ball, or on the *putting green* place the ball, as near as possible to where the article was when the ball came to rest in or on it.

**Exception:** Ball striking person attending *flagstick*—see Rule 17-3b.

(Ball purposely deflected or stopped by opponent or *caddie*—see Rule 1-2.)

19-4 **By Fellow-Competitor, Caddie or Equipment in Stroke Play**

See Rule 19-1 regarding ball deflected by *outside agency.*

19-5 **By Another Ball**

a. **At Rest**

If a player's ball in motion after a *stroke* is deflected or stopped by a *ball in play* and at rest, the player shall play his ball as it lies. In match play, no penalty is incurred. In stroke play, there is no penalty unless both balls lay on the *putting green* prior to the *stroke,* in which case the player incurs a penalty of two strokes.

b. **In Motion**

If a player's ball in motion after a *stroke* is deflected or stopped by another ball in motion after a *stroke,* the player shall play his ball as it lies. There is no penalty unless the player was in breach of Rule 16-1f, in which case he shall incur the penalty for breach of that Rule.

**Exception:** If the player's ball is in motion after a *stroke* on the *putting green* and the other ball in motion is an *outside agency*—see Rule 19-1b.

> PENALTY FOR BREACH OF RULE:
> Match play—Loss of hole;
> Stroke play—Two strokes.

## *Relief Situations and Procedure*

**Rule 20**   **Lifting, Dropping and Placing; Playing from Wrong Place**

**20-1**   **Lifting and Marking**

A ball to be lifted under the *Rules* may be lifted by the player, his *partner* or another person authorized by the player. In any such case, the player shall be responsible for any breach of the *Rules*.

The position of the ball shall be marked before it is lifted under a *Rule* which requires it to be replaced. If it is not marked, the player shall incur a penalty of one stroke and the ball shall be replaced. If it is not replaced, the player shall incur the general penalty for breach of this Rule but no additional penalty under Rule 20-1 shall be applied.

If a ball or ball-marker is accidentally *moved* in the process of lifting the ball under a *Rule* or marking its position, the ball or the ball-marker shall be replaced. There is no penalty provided the movement of the ball or the ball-marker is directly attributable to the specific act of marking the position of or lifting the ball. Otherwise, the player shall incur a *penalty stroke* under this Rule or Rule 18-2a.

**Exception:** If a player incurs a penalty for failing to act in accordance with Rule 5-3 or 12-2, no additional penalty under Rule 20-1 shall be applied.

**Note:** The position of a ball to be lifted should be marked by placing a ball-marker, a small coin or other similar object immediately behind the ball. If the ball-marker interferes with the play, *stance* or *stroke* of another player, it should be placed one or more clubhead-lengths to one side.

## 20-2 Dropping and Re-dropping

### a. By Whom and How

A ball to be dropped under the *Rules* shall be dropped by the player himself. He shall stand erect, hold the ball at shoulder height and arm's length and drop it. If a ball is dropped by any other person or in any other manner and the error is not corrected as provided in Rule 20-6, the player shall incur a *penalty stroke.*

If the ball touches the player, his *partner*, either of their *caddies* or their *equipment* before or after it strikes a part of the *course*, the ball shall be re-dropped, without penalty. There is no limit to the number of times a ball shall be re-dropped in such circumstances.

(Taking action to influence position or movement of ball—see Rule 1-2.)

## b. Where to Drop

When a ball is to be dropped as near as possible to a specific spot, it shall be dropped not nearer the *hole* than the specific spot which, if it is not precisely known to the player, shall be estimated.

A ball when dropped must first strike a part of the *course* where the applicable *Rule* requires it to be dropped. If it is not so dropped, Rules 20-6 and -7 apply.

## c. When to Re-Drop

A dropped ball shall be re-dropped without penalty if it:

(i)   rolls into and comes to rest in a *hazard*;

(ii)  rolls out of and comes to rest outside a *hazard*;

(iii) rolls onto and comes to rest on a *putting green*;

(iv)  rolls and comes to rest *out of bounds*;

(v)   rolls to and comes to rest in a position where there is interference by the condition from which relief was taken under Rule 24-2 (immovable *obstruction*), Rule 25-1 (*abnormal ground conditions*), Rule 25-3 (*wrong putting green*) or a Local Rule (Rule 33-8a), or rolls back into the pitchmark from which it was lifted under Rule 25-2 (embedded ball);

(vi)  rolls and comes to rest more than two club-lengths from where it first struck a part of the *course;*

(vii) rolls and comes to rest nearer the *hole* than:

(a) its original position or estimated position (see Rule 20-2b) unless otherwise permitted by the *Rules;* or

(b) the *nearest point of relief* or maximum available relief (Rule 24-2, 25-1 or 25-3); or

(c) the point where the original ball last crossed the margin of the *water hazard* or *lateral water hazard* (Rule 26-1).

If the ball when re-dropped rolls into any position listed above, it shall be placed as near as possible to the spot where it first struck a part of the *course* when re-dropped.

If a ball to be re-dropped or placed under this Rule is not immediately recoverable, another ball may be substituted.

**Note:** If a ball when dropped or re-dropped comes to rest and subsequently *moves*, the ball shall be played as it lies, unless the provisions of any other *Rule* apply.

## 20-3 Placing and Replacing

### a. By Whom and Where

A ball to be placed under the *Rules* shall be placed by the player or his *partner*. If a ball is to be replaced, the player, his *partner* or the person who lifted or *moved* it shall place it on the spot from which it was lifted or *moved*. In any such case, the player shall be responsible for any breach of the Rules.

If a ball or ball-marker is accidentally *moved* in the process of placing or replacing the ball, the ball or the ball-marker shall be replaced. There is no penalty provided the movement of the ball or the ball-marker is directly attributable to the specific act of placing or replacing the ball or removing the ball-marker. Otherwise, the player shall incur a *penalty stroke* under Rule 18-2a or 20-1.

**b. Lie of Ball to Be Placed or Replaced Altered**

If the original lie of a ball to be placed or replaced has been altered:

(i) except in a *hazard*, the ball shall be placed in the nearest lie most similar to the original lie which is not more than one club-length from the original lie, not nearer the *hole* and not in a *hazard;*

(ii) in a *water hazard,* the ball shall be placed in accordance with Clause (i) above, except that the ball must be placed in the *water hazard;*

(iii) in a *bunker*, the original lie shall be recreated as nearly as possible and the ball shall be placed in that lie.

**c. Spot Not Determinable**

If it is impossible to determine the spot where the ball is to be placed or replaced:

(i) *through the green*, the ball shall be dropped as near as possible to the place where it lay but not in a *hazard* or on a *putting green;*

(ii) in a *hazard*, the ball shall be dropped in the *hazard* as near as possible to the place where it lay;

(iii) on the *putting green,* the ball shall be

placed as near as possible to the place where it lay but not in a *hazard*.

### d. Ball Fails to Come to Rest on Spot

If a ball when placed fails to come to rest on the spot on which it was placed, it shall be replaced without penalty.

If it still fails to come to rest on that spot:

(i) except in a *hazard*, it shall be placed at the nearest spot where it can be placed at rest which is not nearer the *hole* and not in a *hazard;*

(ii) in a *hazard*, it shall be placed in the *hazard* at the nearest spot where it can be placed at rest which is not nearer the *hole*.

If a ball when placed comes to rest on the spot on which it is placed, and it subsequently *moves*, there is no penalty and the ball shall be played as it lies, unless the provisions of any other *Rule* apply.

> PENALTY FOR BREACH OF RULE 20-1, -2 or -3:
> Match play—Loss of hole;
> Stroke play—Two strokes.

### 20-4 When Ball Dropped or Placed Is in Play

If the player's *ball in play* has been lifted, it is again in play when dropped or placed.

A substituted ball becomes the *ball in play* when it has been dropped or placed.

(Ball incorrectly substituted—see Rule 15-1.)

(Lifting ball incorrectly substituted, dropped or placed—see Rule 20-6.)

20-5   **Playing Next Stroke from Where Previous Stroke Played**

When, under the *Rules*, a player elects or is required to play his next *stroke* from where a previous *stroke* was played, he shall proceed as follows: If the *stroke* is to be played from the *teeing ground*, the ball to be played shall be played from anywhere within the *teeing ground* and may be teed; if the *stroke* is to be played from *through the green* or a *hazard*, it shall be dropped; if the *stroke* is to be played on the *putting green,* it shall be placed.

> PENALTY FOR BREACH OF RULE 20-5:
> Match play—Loss of hole;
> Stroke play—Two strokes.

20-6   **Lifting Ball Incorrectly Substituted, Dropped or Placed**

A ball incorrectly substituted, dropped or placed in a wrong place or otherwise not in accordance with the *Rules* but not played may be lifted, without penalty, and the player shall then proceed correctly.

20-7   **Playing from Wrong Place**

For a ball played from outside the *teeing ground* or from a wrong *teeing ground*—see Rule 11-4 and -5.

**a. Match Play**

If a player plays a *stroke* with a ball which has been dropped or placed in a wrong place, he shall lose the hole.

### b. Stroke Play

If a *competitor* plays a *stroke* with his *ball in play* (i) which has been dropped or placed in a wrong place or (ii) which has been *moved* and not replaced in a case where the *Rules* require replacement, he shall, provided a serious breach has not occurred, incur the penalty prescribed by the applicable *Rule* and play out the hole with the ball.

If, after playing from a wrong place, a *competitor* becomes aware of that fact and believes that a serious breach may be involved, he may, provided he has not played a *stroke* from the next *teeing ground* or, in the case of the last hole of the round, left the *putting green,* declare that he will play out the hole with a second ball dropped or placed in accordance with the *Rules*. The *competitor* shall report the facts to the *Committee* before returning his score card; if he fails to do so, he shall be disqualified. The *Committee* shall determine whether a serious breach of the Rule occurred. If so, the score with the second ball shall count and the *competitor* shall add two *penalty strokes* to his score with that ball.

If a serious breach has occurred and the *competitor* has failed to correct it as prescribed above, he shall be disqualified.

**Note:** If a *competitor* plays a second ball, *penalty strokes* incurred solely by playing the ball ruled not to count and *strokes* subsequently taken with that ball shall be disregarded.

**Rule 21**  **Cleaning Ball**

A ball on the *putting green* may be cleaned when lifted under Rule 16-1b. Elsewhere, a ball may be cleaned when lifted except when it has been lifted:

a. To determine if it is unfit for play (Rule 5-3);

b. For identification (Rule 12-2), in which case it may be cleaned only to the extent necessary for identification; or

c. Because it is interfering with or assisting play (Rule 22).

If a player cleans his ball during play of a hole except as provided in this Rule, he shall incur a penalty of one stroke and the ball, if lifted, shall be replaced.

If a player who is required to replace a ball fails to do so, he shall incur the penalty for breach of Rule 20-3a, but no additional penalty under Rule 21 shall be applied.

**Exception:** If a player incurs a penalty for failing to act in accordance with Rule 5-3, 12-2 or 22, no additional penalty under Rule 21 shall be applied.

**Rule 22**  **Ball Interfering with or Assisting Play**

Any player may:

a. Lift his ball if he considers that the ball might assist any other player or

b. Have any other ball lifted if he considers that the ball might interfere with his play or assist the play of any other player,

but this may not be done while another ball is in motion. In stroke play, a player required to lift his ball may play first rather than lift. A ball lifted under this Rule shall be replaced.

> PENALTY FOR BREACH OF RULE:
> Match play—Loss of hole;
> Stroke play—Two strokes.

**Note:** Except on the *putting green*, the ball may not be cleaned when lifted under this Rule - see Rule 21.

## Rule 23  Loose Impediments

### Definition

*"Loose impediments"* are natural objects such as stones, leaves, twigs, branches and the like, dung, worms and insects and casts or heaps made by them, provided they are not fixed or growing, are not solidly embedded and do not adhere to the ball.

Sand and loose soil are *loose impediments* on the *putting green* but not elsewhere.

Snow and natural ice, other than frost, are either *casual water* or *loose impediments,* at the option of the player. Manufactured ice is an *obstruction.*

Dew and frost are not *loose impediments.*

### 23-1  Relief

Except when both the *loose impediment* and the ball lie in or touch the same *hazard,* any *loose impediment* may be removed without penalty. If the ball *moves,* see Rule 18-2c.

When a ball is in motion, a *loose impediment* which might influence the movement of the ball shall not be removed.

PENALTY FOR BREACH OF RULE:
Match play—Loss of hole;
Stroke play —Two strokes.

(Searching for ball in *hazard*—see Rule 12-1.)
(Touching *line of putt*—see Rule 16-1a.)

## Rule 24   Obstructions

### Definitions

The *"nearest point of relief"* is the reference point for taking relief without penalty from interference by an immovable *obstruction* (Rule 24-2), an *abnormal ground condition* (Rule 25-1) or a *wrong putting green* (Rule 25-3).

It is the point on the *course* nearest to where the ball lies, which is not nearer the *hole* and at which, if the ball were so positioned, no interference (as defined) would exist.

**Note:** The player should determine his *nearest point of relief* by using the club with which he expects to play his next *stroke* to simulate the *address* position and swing for such *stroke*.

An *"obstruction"* is anything artificial, including the artificial surfaces and sides of roads and paths and manufactured ice, except:

a. Objects defining *out of bounds,* such as walls, fences, stakes and railings;

b. Any part of an immovable artificial object which is *out of bounds;* and

c. Any construction declared by the *Committee* to be an integral part of the *course.*

---

An *obstruction* is a movable *obstruction* if it may be moved without unreasonable effort, without unduly delaying play and without causing damage. Otherwise it is an immovable *obstruction*.

**Note:** The *Committee* may make a Local Rule declaring a movable *obstruction* to be an immovable *obstruction*.

**24-1  Movable Obstruction**

A player may obtain relief from a movable *obstruction* as follows:

a. If the ball does not lie in or on the *obstruction*, the *obstruction* may be removed. If the ball *moves*, it shall be replaced, and there is no penalty provided that the movement of the ball is directly attributable to the removal of the *obstruction*. Otherwise, Rule 18-2a applies.

b If the ball lies in or on the *obstruction*, the ball may be lifted, without penalty, and the *obstruction* removed. The ball shall *through the green* or in a *hazard* be dropped, or on the *putting green* be placed, as near as possible to the spot directly under the place where the ball lay in or on the *obstruction*, but not nearer the *hole*.

The ball may be cleaned when lifted under Rule 24-1.

When a ball is in motion, an *obstruction* which might influence the movement of the ball, other than an attended *flagstick* or *equipment* of the players, shall not be removed.

(Exerting influence on ball—see Rule 1-2.)

**Note:** If a ball to be dropped or placed under

this Rule is not immediately recoverable, another ball may be substituted.

## 24-2 Immovable Obstruction

### a. Interference

Interference by an immovable *obstruction* occurs when a ball lies in or on the *obstruction*, or so close to the *obstruction* that the *obstruction* interferes with the player's *stance* or the area of his intended swing. If the player's ball lies on the *putting green,* interference also occurs if an immovable *obstruction* on the *putting green* intervenes on his *line of putt*. Otherwise, intervention on the *line of play* is not, of itself, interference under this Rule.

### b. Relief

Except when the ball is in a *water hazard* or a *lateral water hazard*, a player may obtain relief from interference by an immovable obstruction, without penalty, as follows:

- (i) Through the Green: If the ball lies *through the green*, the *nearest point of relief* shall be determined which is not in a *hazard* or on a *putting green*. The player shall lift the ball and drop it within one club-length of and not nearer the *hole* than the *nearest point of relief* on a part of the *course* which avoids interference (as defined) by the immovable *obstruction* and is not in a *hazard* or on a *putting green*.
- (ii) In a *Bunker:* If the ball is in a *bunker*, the player shall lift and drop the ball in accor-

dance with Clause (i) above, except that
the *nearest point of relief* must be in the
*bunker* and the ball must be dropped in
the *bunker*.

(iii) On the *Putting Green:* If the ball lies on
the *putting green,* the player shall lift the
ball and place it at the *nearest point of
relief* which is not in a *hazard*. The *nearest
point of relief* may be off the *putting green*.

The ball may be cleaned when lifted under
Rule 24-2b.

(Ball rolling to a position where there is interference by the condition from which relief was
taken—see Rule 20-2c(v).)

**Exception:** A player may not obtain relief
under Rule 24-2b if (a) it is clearly unreasonable
for him to play a *stroke* because of interference
by anything other than an immovable *obstruction* or (b) interference by an immovable *obstruction* would occur only through use of an unnecessarily abnormal *stance*, swing or direction of
play.

**Note 1:** If a ball is in a *water hazard* (including
a *lateral water hazard*), the player is not entitled
to relief without penalty from interference by an
immovable *obstruction*. The player shall play the
ball as it lies or proceed under Rule 26-1.

**Note 2:** If a ball to be dropped or placed
under this Rule is not immediately recoverable,
another ball may be substituted.

**Note 3:** The *Committee* may make a Local
Rule stating that the player must determine the

*nearest point of relief* without crossing over, through or under the *obstruction.*

### c. Ball Lost

It is a question of fact whether a ball lost after having been struck toward an immovable *obstruction* is lost in the *obstruction.* In order to treat the ball as lost in the *obstruction,* there must be reasonable evidence to that effect. In the absence of such evidence, the ball must be treated as a *lost ball* and Rule 27 applies.

If a ball is *lost* in an immovable *obstruction,* the spot where the ball last entered the *obstruction* shall be determined and, for the purpose of applying this Rule, the ball shall be deemed to lie at this spot.

(i) *Through the Green:* If the ball last entered the immovable *obstruction* at a spot *through the green,* the player may substitute another ball without penalty and take relief as prescribed in Rule 24-2b(i).

(ii) In a *Bunker:* If the ball last entered the immovable *obstruction* at a spot in a *bunker,* the player may substitute another ball without penalty and take relief as prescribed in Rule 24-2b(ii).

(iii) In a *Water Hazard* (including a *Lateral Water Hazard):* If the ball last entered the immovable *obstruction* at a spot in a *water hazard,* the player is not entitled to relief without penalty. The player shall proceed under Rule 26-1.

(iv) On the *Putting Green:* If the ball last entered the immovable *obstruction* at a spot on the *putting green,* the player may substitute another ball without penalty and take relief as prescribed in Rule 24-2b(iii).

> PENALTY FOR BREACH OF RULE:
> Match play—Loss of hole;
> Stroke play—Two strokes.

## Rule 25  Abnormal Ground Conditions, Embedded Ball and Wrong Putting Green

### Definitions

An *"abnormal ground condition"* is any *casual water, ground under repair* or hole, cast or runway on the *course* made by a *burrowing animal,* a reptile or a bird.

A *"burrowing animal"* is an animal that makes a hole for habitation or shelter, such as a rabbit, mole, ground hog, gopher or salamander.

**Note:** A hole made by a non-*burrowing animal,* such as a dog, is not an *abnormal ground condition* unless marked or declared as *ground under repair.*

*"Casual water"* is any temporary accumulation of water on the *course* which is visible before or after the player takes his *stance* and is not in a *water hazard.* Snow and natural ice, other than frost, are *casual water* or *loose impediments,* at the option of the player. Manufactured ice is an *obstruction.* Dew and frost are not *casual water.* A ball is in *casual water* when it lies in or any part of it touches the *casual water.*

*"Ground under repair"* is any part of the *course* so marked by order of the *Committee* or so declared by its authorized representative. It includes material piled for removal and a hole made by a greenkeeper, even if not so marked.

All ground and any grass, bush, tree or other growing thing within the *ground under repair* is part of the *ground under repair.* The margin of *ground under repair* extends vertically downwards, but not upwards. Stakes and lines defining *ground under repair* are in such ground. Such stakes are *obstructions.* A ball is in *ground under repair* when it lies in or any part of it touches the *ground under repair.*

**Note 1:** Grass cuttings and other material left on the *course* which have been abandoned and are not intended to be removed are not *ground under repair* unless so marked.

**Note 2:** The *Committee* may make a Local Rule prohibiting play from *ground under repair* or an environmentally-sensitive area which has been defined as *ground under repair.*

The *"nearest point of relief"* is the reference point for taking relief without penalty from interference by an immovable *obstruction* (Rule 24-2), an *abnormal ground condition* (Rule 25-1) or a *wrong putting green* (Rule 25-3).

It is the point on the *course,* nearest to where the ball lies, which is not nearer the *hole* and at which, if the ball were so positioned, no interference (as defined) would exist.

**Note:** The player should determine his *nearest point of relief* by using the club with which he expects to play his next *stroke* to simulate the address position and swing for such *stroke*.

A *"wrong putting green"* is any *putting green* other than that of the hole being played. Unless otherwise prescribed by the *Committee*, this term includes a practice *putting green* or pitching green on the *course*.

## 25-1 Abnormal Ground Condition

### a. Interference

Interference by an *abnormal ground condition* occurs when a ball lies in or touches the condition or when such a condition interferes with the player's *stance* or the area of his intended swing. If the player's ball lies on the *putting green,* interference also occurs if such condition on the *putting green* intervenes on his *line of putt.* Otherwise, intervention on the *line of play* is not, of itself, interference under this *Rule.*

**Note:** The *Committee* may make a Local Rule denying the player relief from interference with his *stance* by an *abnormal ground condition.*

### b. Relief

Except when the ball is in a *water hazard* or a *lateral water hazard,* a player may obtain relief from interference by an *abnormal ground condition* as follows:

(i) *Through the Green:* If the ball lies *through the green,* the *nearest point of relief* shall be determined which is not in a *hazard* or on a *putting green*. The player shall lift the ball and drop it without penalty within one club-length of and not nearer the *hole* than the *nearest point of relief,* on a part of the *course* which avoids interference (as defined) by the condition and is not in a *hazard* or on a *putting green*.

(ii) In a *Bunker:* If the ball is in a *bunker,* the player shall lift and drop the ball either:

(a) Without penalty, in accordance with Clause (i) above, except that the *nearest point of relief* must be in the *bunker* and the ball must be dropped in the *bunker,* or if complete relief is impossible, in the *bunker* as near as possible to the spot where the ball lay, but not nearer the *hole,* on a part of the *course* which affords maximum available relief from the condition; or

(b) Under penalty of one stroke, outside the *bunker* keeping the point where the ball lay directly between the *hole* and the spot on which the ball is dropped, with no limit to how far behind the *bunker* the ball may be dropped.

(iii) On the *Putting Green:* If the ball lies on the *putting green,* the player shall lift the ball and place it without penalty at the *nearest point of relief* which is not in a *hazard,* or if complete relief is impossible, at the nearest position to where it lay which affords maximum available relief from the condition, but not nearer the *hole* nor in a *hazard*. The *nearest point of relief* or maximum available relief may be off the *putting green*.

The ball may be cleaned when lifted under Rule 25-1b.

(Ball rolling to a position where there is interference by the condition from which relief was taken—see Rule 20-2c(v)).

**Exception:** A player may not obtain relief under Rule 25-1b if (a) it is clearly unreasonable for him to play a *stroke* because of interference by anything other than a condition covered by Rule 25-1a or (b) interference by such a condition would occur only through use of an unnecessarily abnormal *stance*, swing or direction of play.

**Note 1:** If a ball is in a *water hazard* (including a *lateral water hazard*), the player is not entitled to relief without penalty from interference by an *abnormal ground condition*. The player shall play the ball as it lies (unless prohibited by Local Rule) or proceed under Rule 26-1.

**Note 2:** If a ball to be dropped or placed under this Rule is not immediately recoverable, another ball may be substituted.

c. **Ball Lost**

It is a question of fact whether a ball *lost* after having been struck toward an *abnormal ground condition* is *lost* in such condition. In order to treat the ball as *lost* in the *abnormal ground condition,* there must be reasonable evidence to that effect. In the absence of such evidence, the ball must be treated as a *lost ball* and Rule 27 applies.

If a ball is *lost* in an *abnormal ground condition,* the spot where the ball last entered the condition shall be determined and, for the purpose of applying this Rule, the ball shall be deemed to lie at this spot.

(i) *Through the Green:* If the ball last entered the *abnormal ground condition* at a spot *through the green,* the player may substitute another ball without penalty and take relief as prescribed in Rule 25-1b(i).

(ii) In a *Bunker:* If the ball last entered the *abnormal ground condition* at a spot in a *bunker,* the player may substitute another ball without penalty and take relief as prescribed in Rule 25-1b(ii).

(iii) In a *Water Hazard* (including a *Lateral Water Hazard):* If the ball last entered the *abnormal ground condition* at a spot in a *water hazard,* the player is not entitled to relief without penalty. The player shall proceed under Rule 26-1.

(iv) On the *Putting Green:* If the ball last entered the *abnormal ground condition* at a spot on the *putting green,* the player may substitute another ball without penalty and take relief as prescribed in Rule 25-1b(iii).

### 25-2 Embedded Ball

A ball embedded in its own pitch-mark in the ground in any closely-mown area *through the green* may be lifted, cleaned and dropped, without penalty, as near as possible to the spot where it lay but not nearer the *hole*. The ball when dropped must first strike a part of the *course through the green*. "Closely-mown area" means any area of the *course*, including paths through the rough, cut to fairway height or less.

### 25-3 Wrong Putting Green

#### a. Interference

Interference by a *wrong putting green* occurs when a ball is on the *wrong putting green*.

Interference to a player's *stance* or the area of his intended swing is not, of itself, interference under this Rule.

#### b. Relief

If a player has interference by a *wrong putting green,* the player must take relief, without penalty, as follows:

The *nearest point of relief* shall be determined which is not in a *hazard* or on a *putting green*. The player shall lift the ball and drop it within one club-length of and not nearer the *hole* than the *nearest point of relief,* on a part of the *course* which avoids interference (as defined) by the *wrong putting green* and is not in a *hazard* or on a *putting green*. The ball may be cleaned when so lifted.

PENALTY FOR BREACH OF RULE:
Match play—Loss of hole;
Stroke play—Two strokes.

## Rule 26    Water Hazards (Including Lateral Water Hazards)

### Definitions

A *"water hazard"* is any sea, lake, pond, river, ditch, surface drainage ditch or other open water course (whether or not containing water) and anything of a similar nature.

All ground or water within the margin of a *water hazard* is part of the *water hazard*. The margin of a *water hazard* extends vertically upwards and downwards. Stakes and lines defining the margins of *water hazards* are in the *hazards*. Such stakes are *obstructions*. A ball is in a *water hazard* when it lies in or any part of it touches the *water hazard*.

> **Note 1:** Water hazards (other than *lateral water hazards*) should be defined by yellow stakes or lines.

> **Note 2:** The *Committee* may make a Local Rule prohibiting play from an environmentally-sensitive area which has been defined as a *water hazard*.

A *"lateral water hazard"* is a *water hazard* or that part of a *water hazard* so situated that it is not possible or is deemed by the *Committee* to be impracticable to drop a ball behind the *water hazard* in accordance with Rule 26-1b.

That part of a *water hazard* to be played as a *lateral water hazard* should be distinctively marked. A ball is in a *lateral water hazard* when it lies in or any part of it touches the *lateral water hazard*.

**Note 1:** *Lateral water hazards* should be defined by red stakes or lines.

**Note 2:** The *Committee* may make a Local Rule prohibiting play from an environmentally-sensitive area which has been defined as a *lateral water hazard*.

**Note 3:** The *Committee* may define a *lateral water hazard* as a *water hazard*.

**26-1 Ball in Water Hazard**

It is a question of fact whether a ball lost after having been struck toward a *water hazard* is lost inside or outside the *hazard*. In order to treat the ball as lost in the *hazard*, there must be reasonable evidence that the ball lodged in it. In the absence of such evidence, the ball must be treated as a *lost ball* and Rule 27 applies.

If a ball is in or is lost in a *water hazard* (whether the ball lies in water or not), the player may under penalty of one stroke:

a. Play a ball as nearly as possible at the spot from which the original ball was last played (see Rule 20-5); or

b. Drop a ball behind the *water hazard,* keeping the point at which the original ball last crossed the margin of the *water hazard* directly between the *hole* and the spot on which the ball is dropped, with no limit to how far behind the *water hazard* the ball may be dropped; or

c. As additional options available only if the ball last crossed the margin of a *lateral water hazard,* drop a ball outside the *water hazard* within two club-lengths of and not nearer the *hole* than (i) the point where the original ball last crossed the margin of the *water hazard* or (ii) a point on the opposite margin of the *water hazard* equidistant from the *hole.*

The ball may be cleaned when lifted under this Rule.

(Ball moving in water in a *water hazard*—see Rule 14-6.)

## 26-2 Ball Played Within Water Hazard

### a. Ball Comes To Rest in The Hazard

If a ball played from within a *water hazard* comes to rest in the same *hazard* after the *stroke,* the player may:

(i) proceed under Rule 26-1; or

(ii) under penalty of one stroke, play a ball as nearly as possible at the spot from which the last *stroke* from outside the *hazard* was played (see Rule 20-5).

If the player proceeds under Rule 26-1a, he may elect not to play the dropped ball. If he so elects, he may:

(a) Proceed under Rule 26-1b, adding the additional penalty of one stroke prescribed by that Rule; or

(b) Proceed under Rule 26-1c, if applicable, adding the additional penalty of one stroke prescribed by that Rule; or

(c) Add an additional penalty of one stroke and play a ball as nearly as possible at the spot from which the last *stroke* from outside the *hazard* was played (see Rule 20-5).

### b. Ball Lost or Unplayable Outside Hazard or Out of Bounds

If a ball played from within a *water hazard* is lost or declared unplayable outside the *hazard* or is *out of bounds*, the player, after taking a penalty of one stroke under Rule 27-1 or 28a, may:

   (i)   play a ball as nearly as possible at the spot in the *hazard* from which the original ball was last played (see Rule 20-5); or

  (ii)   proceed under Rule 26-1b, or if applicable Rule 26-1c, adding the additional penalty of one stroke prescribed by the Rule and using as the reference point the point where the original ball last crossed the margin of the *hazard* before it came to rest in the *hazard*; or

 (iii)   add an additional penalty of one stroke and play a ball as nearly as possible at the spot from which the last *stroke* from outside the *hazard* was played (see Rule 20-5).

**Note 1:** When proceeding under Rule 26-2b, the player is not required to drop a ball under Rule 27-1 or 28a. If he does drop a ball, he is not required to play it. He may alternatively proceed under Clause (ii) or (iii).

**Note 2:** If a ball played from within a *water hazard* is declared unplayable outside the *hazard*, nothing in Rule 26-2b precludes the player from proceeding under Rule 28b or c.

> PENALTY FOR BREACH OF RULE:
> Match play—Loss of hole;
> Stroke play —Two strokes.

### Rule 27  Ball Lost or Out of Bounds; Provisional Ball

**Definitions**

A ball is *"lost"* if:

a. It is not found or identified as his by the player within five minutes after the player's *side* or his or their *caddies* have begun to search for it; or

b. The player has put another ball into play under the *Rules*, even though he may not have searched for the original ball; or

c. The player has played any stroke with a *provisional ball* from the place where the original ball is likely to be or from a point nearer the *hole* than that place, whereupon the *provisional ball* becomes the *ball in play*.

Time spent in playing a *wrong ball* is not counted in the five-minute period allowed for search.

*"Out of bounds"* is beyond the boundaries of the *course* or any part of the *course* so marked by the *Committee*.

When *out of bounds* is defined by reference to stakes or a fence, or as being beyond stakes or a fence, the *out of bounds* line is determined by the nearest inside points of the stakes or fence posts at ground level excluding angled supports.

Objects defining *out of bounds* such as walls, fences, stakes and railings, are not *obstructions* and are deemed to be fixed.

---

When *out of bounds* is defined by a line on the ground, the line itself is *out of bounds.*

The *out of bounds* line extends vertically upwards and downwards.

A ball is *out of bounds* when all of it lies *out of bounds.*

A player may stand *out of bounds* to play a ball lying within bounds.

A *"provisional ball"* is a ball played under Rule 27-2 for a ball which may be *lost* outside a *water hazard* or may be *out of bounds.*

## 27-1 Ball Lost or Out of Bounds

If a ball is *lost* or is *out of bounds,* the player shall play a ball, under penalty of one stroke, as nearly as possible at the spot from which the original ball was last played (see Rule 20-5).

**Exceptions:**

1. If there is reasonable evidence that the original ball is *lost* in a *water hazard,* the player shall proceed in accordance with Rule 26-1.

2. If there is reasonable evidence that the original ball is *lost* in an immovable *obstruction* (Rule 24-2c) or an *abnormal ground condition* (Rule 25-1c) the player may proceed under the applicable *Rule.*

> PENALTY FOR BREACH OF RULE 27-1:
> Match play—Loss of hole;
> Stroke play—Two strokes.

## 27-2 Provisional Ball

### a. Procedure

If a ball may be *lost* outside a *water hazard* or may be *out of bounds,* to save time the player may play another ball provisionally in accordance with Rule 27-1. The player shall inform his opponent in match play or his *marker* or a *fellow-competitor* in stroke play that he intends to play a *provisional ball,* and he shall play it before he or his *partner* goes forward to search for the original ball.

If he fails to do so and plays another ball, such ball is not a *provisional ball* and becomes the *ball in play* under penalty of stroke and distance (Rule 27-1); the original ball is deemed to be *lost.*

(Order of play from *teeing ground*—see Rule 10-3.)

### b. When Provisional Ball Becomes Ball in Play

The player may play a *provisional ball* until he reaches the place where the original ball is likely to be. If he plays a *stroke* with the *provisional ball* from the place where the original ball is likely to be or from a point nearer the *hole* than that place, the original ball is deemed to be *lost* and the *provisional ball* becomes the *ball in play* under penalty of stroke and distance (Rule 27-1).

If the original ball is *lost* outside a *water hazard* or is *out of bounds,* the *provisional ball* becomes the *ball in play,* under penalty of stroke and distance (Rule 27-1).

If there is reasonable evidence that the original ball is *lost* in a *water hazard,* the player shall proceed in accordance with Rule 26-1.

**Exception:** If there is reasonable evidence that the original ball is *lost* in an immovable *obstruction* (Rule 24-2c) or an *abnormal ground condition* (Rule 25-1c), the player may proceed under the applicable Rule.

### c. When Provisional Ball to Be Abandoned

If the original ball is neither *lost* nor *out of bounds,* the player shall abandon the *provisional ball* and continue play with the original ball. If he fails to do so, any further *strokes* played with the *provisional ball* shall constitute playing a *wrong ball* and the provisions of Rule 15 shall apply.

**Note:** *Strokes* taken and *penalty strokes* incurred solely in playing a *provisional ball* subsequently abandoned under Rule 27-2c shall be disregarded.

## Rule 28   Ball Unplayable

The player may declare his ball unplayable at any place on the *course* except when the ball is in a *water hazard.* The player is the sole judge as to whether his ball is unplayable.

If the player deems his ball to be unplayable, he shall, under penalty of one stroke:

a. Play a ball as nearly as possible at the spot from which the original ball was last played (see Rule 20-5); or

b. Drop a ball within two club-lengths of the spot where the ball lay, but not nearer the *hole*; or

c. Drop a ball behind the point where the ball lay, keeping that point directly between the *hole* and the spot on which the ball is dropped, with no limit to how far behind that point the ball may be dropped.

If the unplayable ball is in a *bunker*, the player may proceed under Clause a, b or c. If he elects to proceed under Clause b or c, a ball must be dropped in the *bunker*.

The ball may be cleaned when lifted under this Rule.

> PENALTY FOR BREACH OF RULE:
> Match play—Loss of hole;
> Stroke play—Two strokes.

## *Other Forms of Play*

**Rule 29**    Threesomes and Foursomes

### Definitions

Threesome: A match in which one plays against two, and each *side* plays one ball.

Foursome: A match in which two play against two, and each *side* plays one ball.

### 29-1   General

In a threesome or a foursome, during any *stipulated round* the *partners* shall play alternately from the *teeing grounds* and alternately during the play of each hole. *Penalty strokes* do not affect the order of play.

### 29-2   Match Play

If a player plays when his *partner* should have played, his *side* shall lose the hole.

### 29-3   Stroke Play

If the *partners* play a *stroke* or *strokes* in incorrect order, such *stroke* or *strokes* shall be cancelled and the *side* shall incur a penalty of two strokes. The *side* shall correct the error by playing a ball in correct order as nearly as possible at the spot from which it first played in incorrect order (see Rule 20-5). If the *side* plays a *stroke* from the next *teeing ground* without first correcting the error or, in the case of the last hole of the round, leaves the *putting green* without declaring its intention to correct the error, the *side* shall be disqualified.

**Rule 30**  **Three-Ball, Best-Ball and Four-Ball Match Play**

**Definitions**

Three-Ball: A match play competition in which three play against one another, each playing his own ball. Each player is playing two distinct *matches*.

Best-Ball: A match in which one plays against the better ball of two or the best ball of three players.

Four-Ball: A match in which two play their better ball against the better ball of two other players.

**30-1**  **Rules of Golf Apply**

The Rules of Golf, so far as they are not at variance with the following special Rules, shall apply to three-ball, best-ball and four-ball *matches*.

**30-2**  **Three-Ball Match Play**

**a. Ball at Rest Moved by an Opponent**

Except as otherwise provided in the *Rules*, if the player's ball is touched or *moved* by an opponent, his *caddie* or *equipment* other than during search, Rule 18-3b applies. That opponent shall incur a *penalty stroke* in his match with the player, but not in his match with the other opponent.

**b. Ball Deflected or Stopped by an Opponent Accidentally**

If a player's ball is accidentally deflected or stopped by an opponent, his *caddie* or *equipment*, no penalty shall be incurred. In his match with that opponent the player may play the ball as it lies or, before another *stroke* is played by either *side*, he may cancel the *stroke* and play a ball without penalty as nearly as possible at the spot from which the original ball was last played (see Rule 20-5). In his match with the other opponent, the ball shall be played as it lies.

**Exception:** Ball striking person attending *flagstick*—see Rule 17-3b.

(Ball purposely deflected or stopped by opponent—see Rule 1-2.)

### 30-3 Best-Ball and Four-Ball Match Play

#### a. Representation of Side

A *side* may be represented by one *partner* for all or any part of a match; all *partners* need not be present. An absent *partner* may join a match between holes, but not during play of a hole.

#### b. Maximum of Fourteen Clubs

The *side* shall be penalized for a breach of Rule 4-4 by any *partner*.

#### c. Order of Play

Balls belonging to the same *side* may be played in the order the *side* considers best.

#### d. Wrong Ball

If a player plays a *stroke* with a *wrong ball* except in a *hazard*, he shall be disqualified for that hole, but his *partner* incurs no penalty even if the *wrong ball* belongs to him. If the *wrong ball* belongs to another player, its owner shall place a ball on the spot from which the *wrong ball* was first played.

### e. Disqualification of Side

(i) A *side* shall be disqualified for a breach of any of the following by any *partner:*

Rule 1-3—Agreement to Waive Rules.

Rule 4-1 or -2—Clubs.

Rule 5-1 or -2—The Ball.

Rule 6-2a—Handicap (playing off higher handicap).

Rule 6-4—*Caddie.*

Rule 6-7—Undue Delay; Slow Play (repeated offense).

Rule 14-3—Artificial Devices and Unusual Equipment.

(ii) A *side* shall be disqualified for a breach of any of the following by all *partners:*

Rule 6-3—Time of Starting and Groups.

Rule 6-8—Discontinuance of Play.

### f. Effect of Other Penalties

If a player's breach of a *Rule* assists his *partner's* play or adversely affects an opponent's play, the *partner* incurs the applicable penalty in addition to any penalty incurred by the player.

In all other cases where a player incurs a penalty for breach of a *Rule*, the penalty shall not apply to his *partner*. Where the penalty is stated to be loss of hole, the effect shall be to disqualify the player for that hole.

### g. Another Form of Match Played Concurrently

In a best-ball or four-ball match when another form of match is played concurrently, the above special *Rules* shall apply.

## Rule 31  Four-Ball Stroke Play

In four-ball stroke play two *competitors* play as *partners*, each playing his own ball. The lower score of the *partners* is the score for the hole. If one *partner* fails to complete the play of a hole, there is no penalty.

### 31-1  Rules of Golf Apply

The Rules of Golf, so far as they are not at variance with the following special *Rules*, shall apply to four-ball stroke play.

### 31-2  Representation of Side

A *side* may be represented by either *partner* for all or any part of a *stipulated round*; both *partners* need not be present. An absent *competitor* may join his *partner* between holes, but not during play of a hole.

### 31-3  Maximum of Fourteen Clubs

The *side* shall be penalized for a breach of Rule 4-4 by either *partner*.

### 31-4  Scoring

The *marker* is required to record for each hole only the gross score of whichever *partner*'s score is to count. The gross scores to count must be individually identifiable; otherwise the *side* shall be disqualified. Only one of the *partners* need be responsible for complying with Rule 6-6b.

(Wrong score—see Rule 31-7a.)

31-5 **Order of Play**

Balls belonging to the same *side* may be played in the order the *side* considers best.

31-6 **Wrong Ball**

If a *competitor* plays a *stroke* or *strokes* with a *wrong ball* except in a *hazard*, he shall add two *penalty strokes* to his score for the hole and shall then play the correct ball. His *partner* incurs no penalty even if the *wrong ball* belongs to him.

If the *wrong ball* belongs to another *competitor*, its owner shall place a ball on the spot from which the *wrong ball* was first played.

31-7 **Disqualification Penalties**

a. **Breach by One Partner**

A *side* shall be disqualified from the competition for a breach of any of the following by either *partner*:

Rule 1-3—Agreement to Waive Rules.

Rule 3-4—Refusal to Comply with Rule.

Rule 4-1 or -2—Clubs.

Rule 5-1 or -2—The Ball.

Rule 6-2b—Handicap (playing off higher-handicap; failure to record handicap).

Rule 6-4—*Caddie.*

Rule 6-6b—Signing and Returning Card.

Rule 6-6d—Wrong Score for Hole, i.e., when the recorded score of the *partner* whose score is to count is lower than actually taken. If the recorded score of the *partner* whose score is to count is higher than actually taken, it must stand as returned.

Rule 6-7—Undue Delay; Slow Play (repeated offense).

Rule 7-1—Practice Before or Between Rounds.

Rule 14-3—Artificial Devices and Unusual *Equipment*.

Rule 31-4—Gross Scores to Count Not Individually Identifiable.

### b. Breach by Both Partners

A *side* shall be disqualified:

(i)   for a breach by both *partners* of Rule 6-3 (Time of Starting and Groups) or Rule 6-8 (Discontinuance of Play), or

(ii)  if, at the same hole, each *partner* is in breach of a Rule the penalty for which is disqualification from the competition or for a hole.

### c. For the Hole Only

In all other cases where a breach of a *Rule* would entail disqualification, the *competitor* shall be disqualified only for the hole at which the breach occurred.

### 31-8   Effect of Other Penalties

If a *competitor's* breach of a *Rule* assists his *partner's* play, the *partner* incurs the applicable penalty in addition to any penalty incurred by the *competitor*.

In all other cases where a *competitor* incurs a penalty for breach of a *Rule,* the penalty shall not apply to his *partner.*

## Rule 32 Bogey, Par and Stableford Competitions

### 32-1 Conditions

Bogey, par and Stableford competitions are forms of stroke competition in which play is against a fixed score at each hole. The Rules for stroke play, so far as they are not at variance with the following special Rules, apply.

#### a. Bogey and Par Competitions

The reckoning for bogey and par competitions is made as in match play. Any hole for which a *competitor* makes no return shall be regarded as a loss. The winner is the *competitor* who is most successful in the aggregate of holes.

The *marker* is responsible for marking only the gross number of *strokes* for each hole where the *competitor* makes a net score equal to or less than the fixed score.

**Note 1:** Maximum of 14 clubs—Penalties as in match play—see Rule 4-4.

**Note 2:** Undue delay; slow play (Rule 6-7)— The player's score shall be adjusted by deducting one hole from the overall result.

#### b. Stableford Competitions

The reckoning in Stableford competitions is made by points awarded in relation to a fixed score at each hole as follows:

| Hole Played In | Points |
| --- | --- |
| More than one over fixed score or no score returned | 0 |
| One over fixed score | 1 |
| Fixed score | 2 |
| One under fixed score | 3 |
| Two under fixed score | 4 |
| Three under fixed score | 5 |
| Four under fixed score | 6 |

The winner is the *competitor* who scores the highest number of points.

The *marker* shall be responsible for marking only the gross number of *strokes* at each hole where the *competitor*'s net score earns one or more points.

**Note 1:** Maximum of 14 clubs (Rule 4-4)—Penalties applied as follows: From total points scored for the round, deduction of two points for each hole at which any breach occurred; maximum deduction per round: four points.

**Note 2:** Undue delay; slow play (Rule 6-7)—The player's score shall be adjusted by deducting two points from the total points scored for the round.

### 32-2 Disqualification Penalties

#### a. From the Competition

A *competitor* shall be disqualified from the competition for a breach of any of the following:

Rule 1-3—Agreement to Waive Rules.

Rule 3-4—Refusal to Comply with Rule.

Rule 4-1 or -2—Clubs.

Rule 5-1 or -2—The Ball.

Rule 6-2b—Handicap (playing off higher handicap; failure to record handicap).

Rule 6-3—Time of Starting and Groups.

Rule 6-4—*Caddie*.

Rule 6-6b—Signing and Returning Card.

Rule 6-6d—Wrong Score for Hole, except that no penalty shall be incurred when a breach of this Rule does not affect the result of the hole.

Rule 6-7—Undue Delay; Slow Play (repeated offense).

Rule 6-8—Discontinuance of Play.

Rule 7-1—Practice Before or Between Rounds.

Rule 14-3—Artificial Devices and Unusual *Equipment*.

**b. For a Hole**

In all other cases where a breach of a *Rule* would entail disqualification, the *competitor* shall be disqualified only for the hole at which the breach occurred.

# *Administration*

### Rule 33 The Committee

#### 33-1 Conditions; Waiving Rule

The *Committee* shall lay down the conditions under which a competition is to be played.

The *Committee* has no power to waive a Rule of Golf.

Certain special rules governing stroke play are so substantially different from those governing match play that combining the two forms of play is not practicable and is not permitted. The results of *matches* played and the scores returned in these circumstances shall not be accepted.

In stroke play the *Committee* may limit a *referee*'s duties.

#### 33-2 The Course

##### a. Defining Bounds and Margins

The *Committee* shall define accurately:

(i) the *course* and *out of bounds*,
(ii) the margins of *water hazards* and *lateral water hazards*,
(iii) *ground under repair*, and
(iv) *obstructions* and integral parts of the *course*.

##### b. New Holes

New *holes* should be made on the day on which a stroke competition begins and at such other times as the *Committee* considers necessary, provided all *competitors* in a single round play with each *hole* cut in the same position.

**Exception:** When it is impossible for a damaged *hole* to be repaired so that it conforms with the Definition, the *Committee* may make a new *hole* in a nearby similar position.

**Note:** Where a single round is to be played on more than one day, the *Committee* may provide in the conditions of a competition that the *holes* and *teeing grounds* may be differently situated on each day of the competition, provided that, on any one day, all *competitors* play with each *hole* and each *teeing ground* in the same position.

### c. Practice Ground

Where there is no practice ground available outside the area of a competition *course*, the *Committee* should lay down the area on which players may practice on any day of a competition, if it is practicable to do so. On any day of a stroke competition, the *Committee* should not normally permit practice on or to a *putting green* or from a *hazard* of the competition *course*.

### d. Course Unplayable

If the *Committee* or its authorized representative considers that for any reason the *course* is not in a playable condition or that there are circumstances which render the proper playing of the game impossible, it may, in match play or stroke play, order a temporary suspension of play or, in stroke play, declare play null and void and cancel all scores for the round in question. When a round is cancelled, all penalties incurred in that round are cancelled.

(Procedure in discontinuing play—see Rule 6-8.)

### 33-3 Times of Starting and Groups

The *Committee* shall lay down the times of starting and, in stroke play, arrange the groups in which *competitors* shall play.

When a match play competition is played over an extended period, the *Committee* shall lay down the limit of time within which each round shall be completed. When players are allowed to arrange the date of their match within these limits, the *Committee* should announce that the match must be played at a stated time on the last day of the period unless the players agree to a prior date.

### 33-4 Handicap Stroke Table

The *Committee* shall publish a table indicating the order of holes at which handicap strokes are to be given or received.

### 33-5 Score Card

In stroke play, the *Committee* shall issue for each *competitor* a score card containing the date and the *competitor*'s name or, in foursome or four-ball stroke play, the *competitors*' names.

In stroke play, the *Committee* is responsible for the addition of scores and application of the handicap recorded on the card.

In four-ball stroke play, the *Committee* is responsible for recording the better-ball score for each hole and in the process applying the handicaps recorded on the card, and adding the better-ball scores.

In bogey, par and Stableford competitions, the *Committee* is responsible for applying the handicap recorded on the card and determining the result of each hole and the overall result or points total.

## 33-6 Decision of Ties

The *Committee* shall announce the manner, day and time for the decision of a halved match or of a tie, whether played on level terms or under handicap.

A halved match shall not be decided by stroke play. A tie in stroke play shall not be decided by a match.

## 33-7 Disqualification Penalty; Committee Discretion

A penalty of disqualification may in exceptional individual cases be waived, modified or imposed if the *Committee* considers such action warranted.

Any penalty less than disqualification shall not be waived or modified.

## 33-8 Local Rules

### a. Policy

The *Committee* may make and publish Local Rules for abnormal conditions if they are consistent with the policy set forth in Appendix I.

### b. Waiving Penalty

A Rule of Golf shall not be waived by a Local Rule. However, if a *Committee* considers that local abnormal conditions interfere with the proper playing of the game to the extent that it is necessary to make a Local Rule which modifies the Rules of Golf, the Local Rule must be authorized by the USGA.

## Rule 34  Disputes and Decisions

### 34-1  Claims and Penalties

#### a. Match Play

In match play if a claim is lodged with the *Committee* under Rule 2-5, a decision should be given as soon as possible so that the state of the match may, if necessary, be adjusted.

If a claim is not made within the time limit provided by Rule 2-5, it shall not be considered unless it is based on facts previously unknown to the player making the claim and the player making the claim had been given wrong information (Rules 6-2a and 9) by an opponent. In any case, no later claim shall be considered after the result of the match has been officially announced, unless the *Committee* is satisfied that the opponent knew he was giving wrong information.

There is no time limit on applying the disqualification penalty for a breach of Rule 1-3.

#### b. Stroke Play

Except as provided below, in stroke play, no penalty shall be rescinded, modified or imposed after the competition has closed. A competition is deemed to have closed when the result has been officially announced or, in stroke play qualifying followed by match play, when the player has teed off in his first match.

**Exceptions:** A penalty of disqualification shall be imposed after the competition has closed if a *competitor:*

(i)  was in breach of Rule 1-3 (Agreement to Waive Rules); or

(ii) returned a score card on which he had recorded a handicap which, before the competition closed, he knew was higher than that to which he was entitled, and this affected the number of strokes received (Rule 6-2b); or

(iii) returned a score for any hole lower than actually taken (Rule 6-6d) for any reason other than failure to include a penalty which, before the competition closed, he did not know he had incurred; or

(iv) knew, before the competition closed, that he had been in breach of any other *Rule* for which the prescribed penalty is disqualification.

## 34-2 Referee's Decision

If a *referee* has been appointed by the *Committee*, his decision shall be final.

## 34-3 Committee's Decision

In the absence of a *referee*, any dispute or doubtful point on the Rules shall be referred to the *Committee*, whose decision shall be final.

If the *Committee* cannot come to a decision, it shall refer the dispute or doubtful point to the Rules of Golf Committee of the United States Golf Association, whose decision shall be final.

If the dispute or doubtful point has not been referred to the Rules of Golf Committee, the player or players have the right to refer an agreed statement through the Secretary of the Club to the Rules of Golf Committee for an opinion as to the correctness of the decision given. The reply will be sent to the Secretary of the Club or Clubs concerned.

If play is conducted other than in accordance with the Rules of Golf, the Rules of Golf Committee will not give a decision on any question.

# *LOCAL RULES; CONDITIONS OF THE COMPETITION*

## *Part A: Local Rules*

As provided in Rule 33-8a, the *Committee* may make and publish Local Rules for local abnormal conditions if they are consistent with the policy set forth in this Appendix. In addition, detailed information regarding acceptable and prohibited Local Rules is provided in "Decisions on the Rules of Golf" under Rule 33-8.

If local abnormal conditions interfere with the proper playing of the game and the *Committee* considers it necessary to modify a Rule of Golf, authorization from the United States Golf Association must be obtained.

1.  **Defining Bounds and Margins**

     Specifying means used to define *out of bounds, water hazards, lateral water hazards, ground under repair, obstructions* and integral parts of the *course* (Rule 33-2a).

2.  **Water Hazards**

     **a. Lateral Water Hazards**

      Clarifying the status of *water hazards* which may be *lateral water hazards* (Rule 26).

     **b. Provisional Ball**

      Permitting play of a *provisional ball* for a ball which may be in a *water hazard* of such character that if the original ball is not found, there is reasonable evidence that it is *lost* in the *water hazard* and it would be impracticable to determine whether the ball is in the *hazard* or to do so would unduly delay play. The ball shall be played provisionally under any of the available options under Rule 26-1 or any applicable Local Rule. In such a case, if a *provisional ball* is played and the original ball is in a *water hazard,* the player may play the original ball as it lies or continue with the *provisional ball* in play, but he may not proceed under Rule 26-1 with regard to the original ball.

3. **Areas of the Course Requiring Preservation; Environmentally-Sensitive Areas**

    Assisting preservation of the *course* by defining areas, including turf nurseries, young plantations and other parts of the course under cultivation as *"ground under repair"* from which play is prohibited.

    When the *Committee* is required to prohibit play from environmentally-sensitive areas which are on or adjoin the *course*, it should make a Local Rule clarifying the relief procedure.

4. **Temporary Conditions—Mud, Extreme Wetness, Poor Conditions and Protection of Course**

    **a. Lifting an Embedded Ball, Cleaning**

    Temporary conditions which might interfere with proper playing of the game, including mud and extreme wetness, warranting relief for an embedded ball anywhere *through the green* or permitting lifting, cleaning and replacing a ball anywhere *through the green* or on a closely-mown area *through the green*.

    **b. "Preferred Lies" and "Winter Rules"**

    Adverse conditions, including the poor condition of the *course* or the existence of mud, are sometimes so general, particularly during winter months, that the *Committee* may decide to grant relief by temporary Local Rule either to protect the *course* or to promote fair and pleasant play. Such Local Rule shall be withdrawn as soon as the conditions warrant.

5. **Obstructions**

   **a. General**

   Clarifying status of objects which may be *obstructions* (Rule 24).

   Declaring any construction to be an integral part of the *course* and, accordingly, not an *obstruction*, e.g., built-up sides of *teeing grounds, putting greens* and *bunkers* (Rules 24 and 33-2a).

   **b. Stones in Bunkers**

   Allowing the removal of stones in *bunkers* by declaring them to be "movable *obstructions*" (Rule 24-1).

   **c. Roads and Paths**
   
   (i) Declaring artificial surfaces and sides of roads and paths to be integral parts of the *course*, or
   
   (ii) Providing relief of the type afforded under Rule 24-2b from roads and paths not having artificial surfaces and sides if they could unfairly affect play.

   **d. Fixed Sprinkler Heads**

   Providing relief from intervention by fixed sprinkler heads on or within two club-lengths of the *putting green* when the ball lies within two club-lengths of the sprinkler head.

### e. Protection of Young Trees

Providing relief for the protection of young trees.

### f. Temporary Obstructions

Providing relief from interference by temporary *obstructions* (e.g., grandstands, television cables and equipment, etc.).

6. **Dropping Zones (Ball Drops)**

    Establishing special areas on which balls may or shall be dropped when it is not feasible or practicable to proceed exactly in conformity with Rule 24-2b or 24-2c (Immovable *Obstruction*), Rule 25-1b or 25-1c *(Abnormal Ground Conditions)*, Rule 25-3 *(Wrong Putting Green)*, Rule 26-1 *(Water Hazards and Lateral Water Hazards)* or Rule 28 (Ball Unplayable).

# *Part B: Specimen Local Rules*

Within the policy set out in Part A of this Appendix, the *Committee* may adopt a Specimen Local Rule by referring, on a score card or notice board, to the examples given below. However, Specimen Local Rules 3a, 3b, 3c, and 6a and 6b, should not be printed or referred to on a score card as they are all of limited duration.

1. **Areas of the Course Requiring Preservation; Environmentally-Sensitive Areas**

   **a. Ground Under Repair; Play Prohibited**

   If the *Committee* wishes to protect any area of the *course*, it should declare it to be *ground under repair* and prohibit play from within that area. The following Local Rule is recommended:

   > "The _____(defined by ____) is *ground under repair* from which play is prohibited. If a player's ball lies in the area, or if it interferes with the player's *stance* or the area of his intended swing, the player must take relief under Rule 25-1."

   > PENALTY FOR BREACH OF LOCAL RULE:
   > Match play—Loss of hole;
   > Stroke play—Two strokes.

   **b. Environmentally-Sensitive Areas**

   If an appropriate authority (i.e., a Government Agency or the like) prohibits entry into and/or play from an area on or adjoining the course for environmental reasons, the *Committee* should make a Local Rule clarifying the relief procedure.

The *Committee* has some discretion in terms of whether the area is defined as *ground under repair,* a *water hazard* or *out of bounds.* However, it may not simply define such an area to be a *water hazard* if it does not meet the Definition of a *"Water Hazard"* and it should attempt to preserve the character of the hole.

The following Local Rule is recommended:

### "I. Definition

An environmentally-sensitive area is an area so declared by an appropriate authority, entry into and/or play from which is prohibited for environmental reasons. Such an area may be defined as *ground under repair,* a *water hazard,* a *lateral water hazard* or *out of bounds* at the discretion of the *Committee* provided that, in the case of an environmentally-sensitive area which has been defined as a *water hazard* or a *lateral water hazard,* the area is, by Definition, a *water hazard.*

**Note:** The *Committee* may not declare an area to be environmentally-sensitive.

### II. Ball in Environmentally-Sensitive Area

a. *Ground Under Repair*

If a ball is in an environmentally-sensitive area which is defined as *ground under repair,* a ball must be dropped in accordance with Rule 25-1b.

If there is reasonable evidence that

a ball is *lost* within an environmentally-sensitive area which is defined as *ground under repair,* the player may take relief without penalty as prescribed in Rule 25-1c.

**b.** *Water Hazards and Lateral Water Hazards*

If a ball is in or there is reasonable evidence that it is *lost* in an environmentally-sensitive area which is defined as a *water hazard* or *lateral water hazard,* the player must, under penalty of one stroke, proceed under Rule 26-1.

**Note:** If a ball dropped in accordance with Rule 26 rolls into a position where the environmentally-sensitive area interferes with the player's *stance* or the area of his intended swing, the player must take relief as provided in Clause 3 of this Local Rule.

**c.** *Out of Bounds*

If a ball is in an environmentally-sensitive area which is defined as *out of bounds,* the player shall play a ball, under penalty of one stroke, as nearly as possible at the spot from which the original ball was last played (see Rule 20-5).

**III. Interference with Stance or Area of Intended Swing**

Interference by an environmentally-sensitive area occurs when such a condition interferes with the player's stance or the area of his intended swing. If interference exists, the player must take relief as follows:

(i) *Through the Green:* If the ball lies *through the green,* the point on the *course* nearest to where the ball lies shall be determined which (a) is not nearer the *hole,* (b) avoids interference by the condition and (c) is not in a *hazard* or on a *putting green.* The player shall lift the ball and drop it without penalty within one club-length of the point thus determined on a part of the *course* that fulfills (a), (b) and (c) above.

(ii) In a *Hazard:* If the ball is in a *hazard,* the player shall lift the ball and drop it either:

  (a) Without penalty, in the *hazard,* as near as possible to the spot where the ball lay, but not nearer the *hole,* on a part of the *course* which provides complete relief from the condition; or

  (b) Under penalty of one stroke, outside the *hazard,* keeping the point where the ball lay directly between the *hole* and the spot on which the ball is dropped, with no limit to how far behind the *hazard* the ball may be dropped. Additionally, the

player may proceed under Rule 26
or 28 if applicable.

(iii) On the *Putting Green:* If the ball lies
on the *putting green,* the player shall
lift the ball and place it without
penalty in the nearest position to
where it lay which affords complete
relief from the condition, but not
nearer the *hole* or in a *hazard.*

The ball may be cleaned when so lifted
under Clause 3 of this Local Rule.

**Exception:** A player may not obtain relief
under Clause 3 of this Local Rule if (a) it
is clearly unreasonable for him to play a
*stroke* because of interference by anything
other than a condition covered by this
Local Rule or (b) interference by such a
condition would occur only through use
of an unnecessarily abnormal *stance,*
swing or direction of play.

PENALTY FOR BREACH OF LOCAL RULE:
  Match play—Loss of hole;
  Stroke play—Two strokes.

**Note:** In the case of a serious breach of
this Local Rule, the *Committee* may
impose a penalty of disqualification."

## 2. Protection of Young Trees

When it is desired to prevent damage to young
trees, the following Local Rule is recommended:

"Protection of young trees identified by \_\_\_\_\_ . If such a tree interferes with a player's *stance* or the area of his intended swing, the ball must be lifted, without penalty, and dropped in accordance with the procedure prescribed in Rule 24-2b (Immovable *Obstruction*). If the ball lies in a *water hazard,* the player shall lift and drop the ball in accordance with Rule 24-2b(i) except that the *nearest point of relief* must be in the *water hazard* and the ball must be dropped in the *water hazard* or the player may proceed under Rule 26. The ball may be cleaned when so lifted.

**Exception:** A player may not obtain relief under this Local Rule if (a) it is clearly unreasonable for him to play a *stroke* because of interference by anything other than such tree or (b) interference by such tree would occur only through use of an unnecessarily abnormal *stance*, swing or direction of play.

> PENALTY FOR BREACH OF LOCAL RULE:
> Match play—Loss of hole;
> Stroke play—Two strokes."

3. **Temporary Conditions—Mud, Extreme Wetness, Poor Conditions and Protection of the Course**

   **a. Relief for Embedded Ball; Cleaning Ball**
   Rule 25-2 provides relief without penalty for a ball embedded in its own pitch-mark in any closely-mown area *through the green.* On the *putting green,* a ball may be lifted and damage caused by the impact of a ball may be repaired (Rules 16-1b and c). When permission to take

relief for an embedded ball anywhere *through the green* would be warranted, the following Local Rule is recommended:

> *"Through the green,* a ball which is embedded in its own pitch-mark in the ground, other than sand, may be lifted without penalty, cleaned and dropped as near as possible to where it lay but not nearer the *hole.* The ball when dropped must first strike a part of the *course through the green.*

> **Exception:** A player may not obtain relief under this Local Rule if it is clearly unreasonable for him to play a *stroke* because of interference by anything other than the condition covered by this Local Rule.

> PENALTY FOR BREACH OF LOCAL RULE:
> Match play—Loss of hole;
> Stroke play—Two strokes."

Alternatively, conditions may be such that permission to lift, clean and replace the ball will suffice. In such circumstances, the following Local Rule is recommended:

> "(Specify area) a ball may be lifted, cleaned and replaced without penalty.

> **Note:** The position of the ball shall be marked before it is lifted under this Local Rule—see Rule 20-1.

> PENALTY FOR BREACH OF LOCAL RULE:
> Match play—Loss of hole;
> Stroke play—Two strokes."

### b. "Preferred Lies" and "Winter Rules"

The USGA does not endorse "preferred lies" and "winter rules" and recommends that the Rules of Golf be observed uniformly. *Ground under repair* is provided for in Rule 25 and occasional local abnormal conditions which might interfere with fair play and are not widespread should be defined as *ground under repair*.

However, adverse conditions are sometimes so general throughout a *course* that the *Committee* believes "preferred lies" or "winter rules" would promote fair play or help protect the *course*. Heavy snows, spring thaws, prolonged rains or extreme heat can make fairways unsatisfactory and sometimes prevent use of heavy mowing equipment.

When a *Committee* adopts a Local Rule for "preferred lies" or "winter rules" it should be set out in detail and should be interpreted by the *Committee*, as there is no established code for "winter rules." Without a detailed Local Rule, it is meaningless for a *Committee* to post a notice merely saying "Winter Rules Today."

The following Local Rule would seem appropriate for the conditions in question, but the USGA will not interpret it:

"A ball lying on a closely-mown area *through the green* may, without penalty, be moved or may be lifted, cleaned and placed within (specify area, e.g., six inches, one club-length, etc.) of where it originally lay, but not nearer the *hole* and not in a *hazard* or on a *putting green.* A player may move or place his ball once and after the ball has been so moved or placed, it is in play.

> PENALTY FOR BREACH OF LOCAL RULE:
> Match play—Loss of hole;
> |Stroke play—Two strokes."

Before a *Committee* adopts a Local Rule permitting "preferred lies" or "winter rules," the following facts should be considered:

1. Such a Local Rule conflicts with the Rules of Golf and the fundamental principle of playing the ball as it lies.

2. "Winter rules" are sometimes adopted under the guise of protecting the *course* when, in fact, the practical effect is just the opposite—they permit moving the ball to the best turf, from which divots are then taken to injure the *course* further.

3. "Preferred lies" or "winter rules" tend generally to lower scores and handicaps, thus penalizing the players in competition with players whose scores for handicaps are made under the Rules of Golf.

4. Extended use or indiscriminate use of "preferred lies" or "winter rules" will place players at a disadvantage when competing at a *course* where the ball must be played as it lies.

#### c. Aeration Holes

When a *course* has been aerated, a Local Rule permitting relief, without penalty, from an aeration hole may be warranted. The following

Local Rule is recommended:

"*Through the green*, a ball which comes to rest in or on an aeration hole may be lifted without penalty, cleaned and dropped, as near as possible to the spot where it lay but not nearer the *hole*. The ball when dropped must first strike a part of the *course through the green*.

On the *putting green*, the player shall place the ball at the nearest spot not nearer the *hole* which avoids such situation.

> PENALTY FOR BREACH OF LOCAL RULE:
> Match play—Loss of hole;
> Stroke play—Two strokes."

4. **Stones in Bunkers**

Stones are, by definition, *loose impediments* and, when a player's ball is in a *hazard*, a stone lying in or touching the *hazard* may not be touched or moved (Rule 13-4). However, stones in *bunkers* may represent a danger to players (a player could be injured by a stone struck by the player's club in an attempt to play the ball) and they may interfere with the proper playing of the game.

When permission to lift a stone in a *bunker* would be warranted, the following Local Rule is recommended:

"Stones in *bunkers* are movable *obstructions* (Rule 24-1 applies)."

5. **Fixed Sprinkler Heads**

Rule 24-2 provides relief without penalty from interference by an immovable *obstruction*, but it also provides that, except on the *putting green,* intervention on the *line of play* is not, of itself, interference under this Rule.

However, on some courses, the aprons of the *putting greens* are so closely mown that players may wish to putt from just off the green. In such conditions, fixed sprinkler heads on the apron may interfere with the proper playing of the game and the introduction of the following Local Rule providing additional relief without penalty from intervention by a fixed sprinkler head would be warranted:

"All fixed sprinkler heads are immovable *obstructions* and relief from interference by them may be obtained under Rule 24-2. In addition, if a ball lies off the *putting green* but not in a *hazard* and such an *obstruction* on or within two club-lengths of the *putting green* and within two club-lengths of the ball intervenes on the *line of play* between the ball and the *hole*, the player may take relief as follows:

The ball shall be lifted and dropped at the nearest point to where the ball lay which (a) is not nearer the *hole*, (b) avoids such intervention and (c) is not in a *hazard* or on a *putting green.* The ball may be cleaned when so lifted.

PENALTY FOR BREACH OF LOCAL RULE:
Match play—Loss of hole;
Stroke play—Two strokes."

6. **Temporary Obstructions**

When temporary *obstructions* are installed on or adjoining the *course*, the *Committee* should define the status of such *obstructions* as movable, immovable or temporary immovable *obstructions*.

### a. Temporary Immovable Obstructions

If the *Committee* defines such *obstructions* as temporary immovable *obstructions*, the following Local Rule is recommended:

"I. **Definition**

A temporary immovable *obstruction* is a non-permanent artificial object which is often erected in conjunction with a competition and which is fixed or not readily movable.

Examples of temporary immovable *obstructions* include, but are not limited to, tents, scoreboards, grandstands, television towers and lavatories.

Supporting guy wires are part of the temporary immovable *obstruction* unless the *Committee* declares that they are to be treated as elevated power lines or cables.

II. **Interference**

Interference by a temporary immovable *obstruction* occurs when (a) the ball lies in front of and so close to the *obstruction* that the *obstruction* interferes with the player's *stance* or the area of his intended swing, or (b) the ball lies in, on, under or behind the *obstruction* so that any part of the *obstruction* intervenes directly between the player's ball and the *hole*; interference also exists if the ball lies within one club-length of a spot where such intervention would exist.

**Note:** A ball is under a temporary immovable *obstruction* when it is below the outer most edges of the *obstruction*, even if these edges do not extend downwards to the ground.

III. **Relief**

A player may obtain relief from interference by a temporary immovable *obstruction*, including a temporary immovable *obstruction* which is *out of bounds*, as follows:

(a) *Through the Green:* If the ball lies *through the green*, the point on the *course* nearest to where the ball lies shall be determined which (a) is not nearer the *hole*, (b) avoids interference as defined in Clause 2 and (c) is not in a *hazard* or on a *putting green*. The player shall lift the ball and drop it without penalty within one club-length of the point thus determined on a part of the *course* which fulfills (a), (b) and (c) above.

(b) *In a Hazard:* If the ball is in a *hazard*, the player shall lift and drop the ball either:

(i) Without penalty, in the *hazard*, on the nearest part of the *course* affording complete relief within the limits specified in Clause 3a above or, if complete relief is impossible, on a part of the *course* within the *hazard* which affords maximum available relief; or

(ii) Under penalty of one stroke, outside the *hazard* as follows: the point on the *course* nearest to where the ball lies shall be determined which (a) is not nearer the *hole*, (b) avoids interference as defined in Clause 2 and (c) is not in a *hazard*. The player shall drop the ball within one club-length of the point thus determined on a part of the *course* which fulfills (a), (b) and (c) above.

The ball may be cleaned when lifted under Clause 3.

**Note 1:** If the ball lies in a *hazard*, nothing in this Local Rule precludes the player from proceeding under Rule 26 or Rule 28, if applicable.

**Note 2:** If a ball to be dropped under this Local Rule is not immediately recoverable, another ball may be substituted.

**Note 3:** A *Committee* may make a Local Rule (a) permitting or requiring a player to use a dropping zone or ball drop when taking relief from a temporary immovable *obstruction* or (b) permitting a player, as an additional relief option, to drop the ball on the opposite side of the *obstruction* from the point established under Clause 3, but otherwise in accordance with Clause 3.

**Exceptions:** If a player's ball lies in front of or behind the temporary immovable *obstruction* (not in, on or under the *obstruction*) he may not obtain relief under Clause 3 if:

1.  It is clearly unreasonable for him to play a *stroke* or, in the case of intervention, to play a *stroke* such that the ball could finish on a direct line to the *hole*, because of interference by anything other than the temporary immovable *obstruction*;

2.  Interference by the temporary immovable *obstruction* would occur only through use of an unnecessarily abnormal *stance*, swing or direction of play; or

3.  In the case of intervention, it would be clearly unreasonable to expect the player to be able to strike the ball far enough towards the *hole* to reach the temporary immovable *obstruction*.

**Note:** A player not entitled to relief due to these exceptions may proceed under Rule 24-2.

IV. **Ball Lost**

If there is reasonable evidence that the ball is *lost* in, on or under a temporary immovable *obstruction*, a ball may be dropped under the provisions of Clause 3 or Clause 5, if applicable. For the purpose of applying Clauses 3 and 5, the ball shall be deemed to lie at the spot where it last entered the *obstruction* (Rule 24-2c).

V. **Dropping Zones (Ball Drops)**

If the player has interference from a temporary immovable *obstruction*, the *Committee* may permit or require the use of a dropping zone or ball drop. If the player uses a dropping zone in taking relief, he must drop the ball in the dropping zone nearest to where his ball originally lay or is deemed to lie under Clause 4 (even though the nearest dropping zone may be nearer the *hole*).

**Note 1:** A *Committee* may make a Local Rule prohibiting the use of a dropping zone or ball drop which is nearer the *hole*.

**Note 2:** If the ball is dropped in a dropping zone, the ball shall not be re-dropped if it comes to rest within two club-lengths of the spot where it first struck a part of the *course* even though it may come to rest nearer the *hole* or outside the boundaries of the dropping zone.

> PENALTY FOR BREACH OF LOCAL RULE:
> Match play—Loss of hole;
> Stroke play—Two strokes."

## b. Temporary Power Lines and Cables

When temporary power lines, cables, or telephone lines are installed on the *course*, the following Local Rule is recommended:

"Temporary power lines, cables, telephone lines and mats covering or stanchions supporting them are *obstructions:*

1. If they are readily movable, Rule 24-1 applies.

2. If they are fixed or not readily movable, the player may, if the ball lies *through the green* or in a *bunker*, obtain relief as provided in Rule 24-2b. If the ball lies in a *water hazard,* the player may lift and drop the ball in accordance with Rule 24-2b(i) except that the *nearest point of relief* must be in the *water hazard* and the ball must be dropped in the *water hazard* or the player may proceed under Rule 26.

3. If a ball strikes an elevated power line or cable, the stroke shall be cancelled and replayed, without penalty (see Rule 20-5). If the ball is not immediately recoverable another ball may be substituted.

**Note:** Guy wires supporting a temporary immovable *obstruction* are part of the temporary immovable *obstruction* unless the *Committee*, by Local Rule, declares that they are to be treated as elevated power lines or cables.

> **Exception:** Ball striking elevated junction section of cable rising from the ground shall not be replayed.

4. Grass-covered cable trenches are *ground under repair* even if not so marked and Rule 25-1b applies."

# Part C: Conditions of the Competition

Rule 33-1 provides, "The *Committee* shall lay down the conditions under which a competition is to be played." Such conditions should include many matters such as method of entry, eligibility, number of rounds to be played, etc. which it is not appropriate to deal with in the Rules of Golf or this Appendix. Detailed information regarding such conditions is provided in "Decisions on the Rules of Golf" under Rule 33-1.

However, there are seven matters which might be covered in the Conditions of the Competition to which the *Committee*'s attention is specifically drawn by way of a Note to the appropriate Rule. These are:

1. **Specification of the Ball (Note to Rule 5-1)**

The following two conditions are recommended only for competitions involving expert players:

**a. List of Conforming Golf Balls**

The USGA periodically issues a List of Conforming Golf Balls which lists balls that have been tested and found to conform. If the *Committee* wishes to require use of a brand of golf ball on the List, the List should be posted and the following condition of competition used:

"The ball the player uses shall be named on the current List of Conforming Golf Balls issued by the United States Golf Association.

PENALTY FOR BREACH OF CONDITION:
Disqualification."

### b. One Ball Condition

If it is desired to prohibit changing brands and types of golf balls during a *stipulated round,* the following condition is recommended:

"Limitation on Balls Used During Round: (Note to Rule 5-1)

(i) "One Ball" Condition: During a *stipulated round,* the balls a player uses must be of the same brand and type as detailed by a single entry on the current List of Conforming Golf Balls.

PENALTY FOR BREACH OF CONDITION:
Match Play —At the conclusion of the hole at which the breach is discovered, the state of the match shall be adjusted by deducting one hole for each hole at which a breach occurred; maximum deduction per round: Two holes.
Stroke Play —Two strokes for each hole at which any breach occurred; maximum penalty per round: Four strokes.

(ii) Procedure When Breach Discovered: When a player discovers that he has used a ball in breach of this condition, he shall abandon that ball before playing from the next *teeing ground* and complete the round using a proper ball;

otherwise, the player shall be disqualified. If discovery is made during play of a hole and the player elects to substitute a proper ball before completing that hole, the player shall place a proper ball on the spot where the ball used in breach of the condition lay."

2. **Time of Starting (Note to Rule 6-3a)**

   If the *Committee* wishes to act in accordance with the Note, the following wording is recommended:

   "If the player arrives at his starting point, ready to play, within five minutes after his starting time, in the absence of circumstances which warrant waiving the penalty of disqualification as provided in Rule 33-7, the penalty for failure to start on time is loss of the first hole to be played in match play or two strokes in stroke play. Penalty for lateness beyond five minutes is disqualification."

3. **Pace of Play**

   The *Committee* may lay down pace of play guidelines to help prevent slow play, in accordance with Note 2 to Rule 6-7.

4. **Suspension of Play Due to a Dangerous Situation (Note to Rule 6-8b)**

   As there have been many deaths and injuries from lightning on golf courses, all clubs and sponsors of golf competitions are urged to take precautions for the protection of persons against lightning. Attention is called to Rules 6-8 and 33-2d. If the *Committee* desires to adopt the condition in the Note under Rule 6-8b, the following wording is recommended:

"When play is suspended by the *Committee* for a dangerous situation, if the players in a match or group are between the play of two holes, they shall not resume play until the *Committee* has ordered a resumption of play. If they are in the process of playing a hole, they shall discontinue play immediately and shall not thereafter resume play until the *Committee* has ordered a resumption of play. If a player fails to discontinue play immediately, he shall be disqualified unless circumstances warrant waiving such penalty as provided in Rule 33-7.

The signal for suspending play due to a dangerous situation will be a prolonged note of the siren."

The following signals are generally used and it is recommended that all *Committees* do similarly:

**Discontinue Play Immediately:**
   One prolonged note of siren.

**Discontinue Play:** Three consecutive notes of siren, repeated.

**Resume Play:** Two short notes of siren, repeated.

5.  **Practice**

   **a. General**

   The *Committee* may make regulations governing practice in accordance with the Note to Rule 7-1, Exception (c) to Rule 7-2, Note 2 to Rule 7 and Rule 33-2c.

### b. Practice Between Holes (Note 2 to Rule 7)

It is recommended that a condition of competition prohibiting practice putting or chipping on or near the *putting green* of the hole last played be introduced only in stroke play competitions. The following wording is recommended:

"A player shall not play any practice *stroke* on or near the *putting green* of the hole last played. If a practice *stroke* is played on or near the *putting green* of the hole last played, the player shall incur a penalty of two strokes at the next hole, except that in the case of the last hole of the round, he incurs the penalty at that hole."

### 6. Advice in Team Competitions

If the *Committee* wishes to act in accordance with the Note under Rule 8, the following wording is recommended:

"In accordance with the Note to Rule 8 of the Rules of Golf, each team may appoint one person (in addition to the persons from whom *advice* may be asked under that Rule) who may give *advice* to members of that team. Such person (if it desired to insert any restriction on who may be nominated insert such restriction here) shall be identified to the *Committee* before giving *advice*."

### 7. New Holes

The *Committee* may provide, in accordance with the Note to Rule 33-2b, that the *holes* and *teeing grounds* for a single round competition, being held on more than one day, may be differently situated on each day.

Other conditions of the competition might include:

**Transportation**

If it is desired to require players to walk in a competition, the following condition is recommended:

"Players shall walk at all times during a *stipulated round*.

> PENALTY FOR BREACH OF CONDITION:
> Match play—At the conclusion of the hole at which the breach is discovered, the state of the match shall be adjusted by deducting one hole for each hole at which a breach occurred. Maximum deduction per round: Two holes.
>
> Stroke play—Two strokes for each hole at which any breach occurred; maximum penalty per round: Four strokes. In the event of a breach between the play of two holes, the penalty applies to the next hole.
>
> Match or stroke play—Use of any unauthorized form of transportation shall be discontinued immediately upon discovery that a breach has occurred. Otherwise, the player shall be disqualified."

**How to Decide Ties**

Rule 33-6 empowers the *Committee* to determine how and when a halved match or a stroke play tie shall be decided. The decision should be published in advance.

The USGA recommends:

**Match Play**

A match which ends all square should be played off hole by hole until one *side* wins a hole. The play-off should start on the hole where the match began. In a handicap match, handicap strokes should be allowed as in the prescribed round.

**Stroke Play**

(a) In the event of a tie in a scratch stroke play competition, a play-off is recommended. Such a play-off may be over 18 holes or a smaller number of holes as specified by the *Committee*. If that is not feasible or there is still a tie, a hole-by-hole play-off is recommended.

(b) In the event of a tie in a handicap stroke play competition, a play-off with handicaps is recommended. Such a play-off may be over 18 holes or a smaller number of holes as specified by the *Committee*. If the play-off is less than 18 holes the percentage of 18 holes to be played should be applied to the players' handicaps to determine their play-off handicaps. Handicap stroke fractions of one-half stroke or more should count as a full stroke and any lesser fraction should be disregarded.

(c) In either a scratch or handicap stroke play competition, if a play-off of any type is not feasible, matching score cards is recommended. The method of matching cards should be announced in advance. An acceptable method of matching cards is to determine the winner on the basis of the best score for the last nine holes. If the tying players have the same score for the last nine, determine the winner on the basis of the last six holes, last three holes and finally the 18th hole. If such a method is used in a handicap stroke play competition, one-half, one-third, one-sixth, etc. of the handicaps should be deducted. Fractions should not be disregarded. If such a method is used in a competition with a multiple tee start, it is recommended that the "last nine holes, last six holes, etc." is considered to be holes 10-18, 13-18, etc.

(d)  If the conditions of the competition provide that ties shall be decided over the last nine, last six, last three and last hole, they should also provide what will happen if this procedure does not produce a winner.

**Draw for Match Play**

Although the draw for match play may be completely blind or certain players may be distributed through different quarters or eighths, the General Numerical Draw is recommended if matches are determined by a qualifying round.

**General Numerical Draw**

For purposes of determining places in the draw, ties in qualifying rounds other than those for the last qualifying place shall be decided by the order in which scores are returned, with the first score to be returned receiving the lowest available number, etc. If it is impossible to determine the order in which scores are returned, ties shall be determined by a blind draw.

| UPPER HALF | LOWER HALF | UPPER HALF | LOWER HALF |
|---|---|---|---|
| **64 QUALIFIERS** | | **32 QUALIFIERS** | |
| 1 vs. 64 | 2 vs. 63 | 1 vs. 32 | 2 vs. 31 |
| 32 vs. 33 | 31 vs. 34 | 16 vs. 17 | 15 vs. 18 |
| 16 vs. 49 | 15 vs. 50 | 8 vs. 25 | 7 vs. 26 |
| 17 vs. 48 | 18 vs. 47 | 9 vs. 24 | 10 vs. 23 |
| 8 vs. 57 | 7 vs. 58 | 4 vs. 29 | 3 vs. 30 |
| 25 vs. 40 | 26 vs. 39 | 13 vs. 20 | 14 vs. 19 |
| 9 vs. 56 | 10 vs. 55 | 5 vs. 28 | 6 vs. 27 |
| 24 vs. 41 | 23 vs. 42 | 12 vs. 21 | 11 vs. 22 |
| 4 vs. 61 | 3 vs. 62 | **16 QUALIFIERS** | |
| 29 vs. 36 | 30 vs. 35 | 1 vs. 16 | 2 vs.15 |
| 13 vs. 52 | 14 vs. 51 | 8 vs. 9 | 7 vs.10 |
| 20 vs. 45 | 19 vs. 46 | 4 vs. 13 | 3 vs.14 |
| 5 vs. 60 | 6 vs. 59 | 5 vs. 12 | 6 vs. 11 |
| 28 vs. 37 | 27 vs. 38 | **8 QUALIFIERS** | |
| 12 vs. 53 | 11 vs. 54 | 1 vs. 8 | 2 vs. 7 |
| 21 vs. 44 | 22 vs. 43 | 4 vs. 5 | 3 vs. 6 |

# *DESIGN OF CLUBS*

## *Appendices II and III*

Any design in a club or ball which is not covered by Rules 4 and 5 and Appendices II and III, or which might significantly change the nature of the game, will be ruled on by the United States Golf Association.

The dimensions contained in Appendices II and III are referenced in imperial measurements. A metric conversion is also referenced for information, calculated using a conversion rate of 1 inch = 25.4 mm. In the event of any dispute over the conformity of a club or ball, the imperial measurements shall take precedence.

## *Design of Clubs*

A player in doubt as to the conformity of a club should consult the United States Golf Association.

A manufacturer should submit to the United States Golf Association a sample of a club which is to be manufactured for a ruling as to whether the club conforms with the *Rules*. If a manufacturer fails to submit a sample before manufacturing and/or marketing the club, the manufacturer assumes the risk of a ruling that the club does not conform with the *Rules*. Any sample submitted to the United States Golf Association will become its property for reference purposes.

The following paragraphs prescribe general regulations for the design of clubs, together with specifications and interpretations.

Where a club, or part of a club, is required to have some specific property, this means that it must be designed and manufactured with the intention of having that property. The finished club or part must have that property within manufacturing tolerances appropriate to the material used.

1. **Clubs**

    a. **General**

    A club is an implement designed to be used for striking the ball and generally comes in three forms: woods, irons and putters distinguished by shape and intended use. A putter is a club with a loft not exceeding ten degrees designed primarily for use on the *putting green*.

    The club shall not be substantially different from the traditional and customary form and make. The club shall be composed of a shaft and a head. All parts of the club shall be fixed so that the club is one unit, and it shall have no external attachments except as otherwise permitted by the *Rules*.

## b. Adjustability

Woods and irons shall not be designed to be adjustable except for weight. Putters may be designed to be adjustable for weight and some other forms of adjustability are also permitted. All methods of adjustment permitted by the *Rules* require that:

   (i)   the adjustment cannot be readily made;

   (ii)  all adjustable parts are firmly fixed and there is no reasonable likelihood of them working loose during a round; and

   (iii) all configurations of adjustment conform with the *Rules*.

The disqualification penalty for purposely changing the playing characteristics of a club during a *stipulated round* (Rule 4-2a) applies to all clubs including a putter.

## c. Length

The overall length of the club shall be at least 18 inches (457.2 mm) measured from the top of the grip along the axis of the shaft or a straight line extension of it to the sole of the club.

## d. Alignment

When the club is in its normal address position the shaft shall be so aligned that:

   (i)   the projection of the straight part of the shaft on to the vertical plane through the

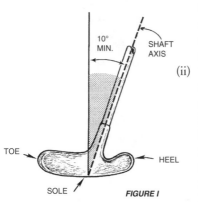

toe and heel shall diverge from the vertical by at least 10 degrees (see Fig I);

(ii) the projection of the straight part of the shaft on to the vertical plane along the intended line of play shall not diverge from the vertical by more than 20 degrees (see Fig. II).

Except for putters, all of the heel portion of the club shall lie within 0.625 inches (15.88 mm) of the plane containing the axis of the straight part of the shaft and the intended (horizontal) line of play (see Fig. III).

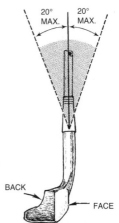

2. **Shaft**

   a. **Straightness**

   The shaft shall be straight from the top of the grip to a point not more than 5 inches (127 mm) above the sole, measured from the point where the shaft ceases to be straight along the axis of the bent part of the shaft and the neck and/or socket (see Fig. IV).

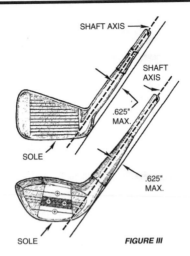

SHAFT AXIS

SHAFT
AXIS

.625"
MAX.

SOLE

.625"
MAX.

SOLE **FIGURE III**

### b. Bending and Twisting Properties

At any point along its length, the shaft shall:

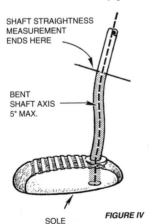

SHAFT STRAIGHTNESS
MEASUREMENT
ENDS HERE

BENT
SHAFT AXIS
5" MAX.

SOLE **FIGURE IV**

(i) bend in such a way that the deflection is the same regardless of how the shaft is rotated about its longitudinal axis; and

(ii) twist the same amount in both directions.

### c. Attachment to Clubhead

The shaft shall be attached to the clubhead at the heel either directly or through a single plain neck and/or socket. The length from the top of the neck and/or socket to the sole of the club shall not exceed 5 inches (127 mm), measured along the axis of, and following any bend in, the neck and/or socket (see Fig. V).

**Exception for Putters:** The shaft or neck or socket of a putter may be fixed at any point in the head.

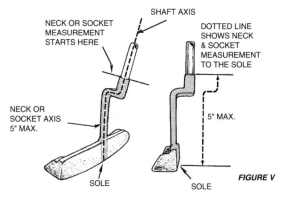

SHAFT AXIS

NECK OR SOCKET
MEASUREMENT
STARTS HERE

DOTTED LINE
SHOWS NECK
& SOCKET
MEASUREMENT
TO THE SOLE

NECK OR
SOCKET AXIS
5" MAX.

5" MAX.

SOLE

SOLE

*FIGURE V*

3. **Grip (see Fig. VI)**

The grip consists of material added to the shaft to enable the player to obtain a firm hold. The grip shall be straight and plain in form, shall extend to the end of the shaft and shall not be molded for any part of the hands. If no material is added, that portion of the shaft designed to be held by the player shall be considered the grip.

(i) For clubs other than putters the grip must be circular in cross-section, except that a continuous, straight, slightly raised rib may be incor-

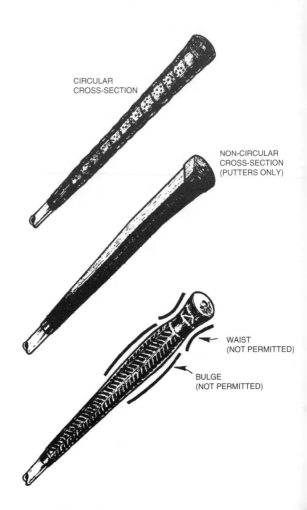

CIRCULAR
CROSS-SECTION

NON-CIRCULAR
CROSS-SECTION
(PUTTERS ONLY)

WAIST
(NOT PERMITTED)

BULGE
(NOT PERMITTED)

*FIGURE*

porated along the full length of the grip, and a slightly indented spiral is permitted on a wrapped grip or a replica of one.

(ii) A putter grip may have a non-circular cross-section, provided the cross-section has no concavity, is symmetrical and remains generally similar throughout the length of the grip. (See Clause (v) below.)

(iii) The grip may be tapered but must not have any bulge or waist. Its cross-sectional dimension measured in any direction must not exceed 1.75 inches (44.45 mm).

(iv) For clubs other than putters the axis of the grip must coincide with the axis of the shaft.

(v) A putter may have two grips provided each is circular in cross-section, the axis of each coincides with the axis of the shaft, and they are separated by at least 1.5 inches (38.1mm).

4. **Clubhead**

   **a. Plain in Shape**

   The clubhead shall be generally plain in shape. All parts shall be rigid, structural in nature and functional. It is not practicable to define plain in shape precisely and comprehensively but features which are deemed to be in breach of this requirement and are therefore not permitted include:

   (i) holes through the head,

   (ii) transparent material added for other than decorative or structural purposes,

---

(iii) appendages to the main body of the head such as knobs, plates, rods or fins, for the purpose of meeting dimensional specifications, for aiming or for any other purpose. Exceptions may be made for putters.

Any furrows in or runners on the sole shall not extend into the face.

### b. Dimensions

The distance from the heel to the toe of the clubhead shall be greater than the distance from the face to the back. These dimensions are measured, with the clubhead in its normal address position, on horizontal lines between vertical projections of the outermost points of (i) the heel and the toe and (ii) the face and the back (see Fig VII, dimension A). If the outermost point of the heel is not clearly defined, it is deemed to be 0.625 inches (15.88mm) above the horizontal plane on which the club is resting in its normal address position (see Fig. VII, dimension B).

### c. Striking Faces

The clubhead shall have only one striking face, except that a putter may have two such faces if their characteristics are the same, and they are opposite each other.

## 5. Club Face

### a. General

The material and construction of, or any treatment to, the face or clubhead shall not have

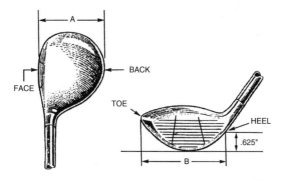

**FIGURE VII**

the effect at impact of a spring (test on file), or impart significantly more spin to the ball than a standard steel face, or have any other effect which would unduly influence the movement of the ball.

The face of the club shall be hard and rigid (some exceptions may be made for putters) and, except for such markings listed below, shall be smooth and shall not have any degree of concavity.

**b. Impact Area Roughness and Material**

Except for markings specified in the following paragraphs, the surface roughness within the area where impact is intended (the "impact area") must not exceed that of decorative sand-blasting, or of fine milling (see Fig. VIII).

The whole of the impact area must be of the same material. Exceptions may be made for wooden clubs.

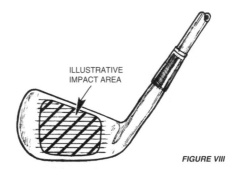

ILLUSTRATIVE
IMPACT AREA

**FIGURE VIII**

### c. Impact Area Markings

Markings in the impact area must not have sharp edges or raised lips as determined by a finger test. Grooves or punch marks in the impact area must meet the following specifications:

(i) **Grooves.** A series of straight grooves with diverging sides and a symmetrical cross-section may be used (see Fig. IX). The width and cross-section must be consistent across the face of the club and along the length of the grooves. Any rounding

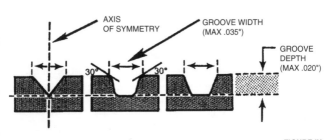

AXIS
OF SYMMETRY

GROOVE WIDTH
(MAX .035")

GROOVE
DEPTH
(MAX .020")

30°        30°

**FIGURE IX**

of groove edges shall be in the form of a radius which does not exceed 0.020 inches (0.508 mm). The width of the grooves shall not exceed 0.035 inches (0.9 mm), using the 30 degree method of measurement on file with the United States Golf Association. The distance between edges of adjacent grooves must not be less than three times the width of a groove, and not less than 0.075 inches (1.905 mm). The depth of a groove must not exceed 0.020 inches (0.508 mm).

**Note:** Exception—see US Decision 4-1/100.

(ii) **Punch Marks.** Punch marks may be used. The area of any such mark must not exceed 0.0044 square inches (2.84 sq. mm). A mark must not be closer to an adjacent mark than 0.168 inches (4.27 mm) measured from center to center. The depth of a punch mark must not exceed 0.040 inches (1.02 mm). If punch marks are used in combination with grooves, a punch mark must not be closer to a groove than 0.168 inches (4.27 mm), measured from center to center.

### d. Decorative Markings

The center of the impact area may be indicated by a design within the boundary of a square whose sides are 0.375 inches (9.53 mm) in length. Such a design must not unduly influence the movement of the ball. Decorative markings are permitted outside the impact area.

### e. Non-metallic Club Face Markings

The above specifications apply to clubs on which the impact area of the face is of metal or a material of similar hardness. They do not apply to clubs with faces made of other materials and whose loft angle is 24 degrees or less, but markings which could unduly influence the movement of the ball are prohibited. Clubs with this type of face and a loft angle exceeding 24 degrees may have grooves of maximum width 0.040 inches (1.02 mm) and maximum depth $1\frac{1}{2}$ times the groove width, but must otherwise conform to the markings specifications above.

### f. Putter Face

The specifications above with regard to roughness, material and markings in the impact area do not apply to putters.

# APPENDIX III
## *THE BALL*

## *The Ball*

### 1. Weight

The weight of the ball shall not be greater than 1.620 ounces avoirdupois (45.93 gm).

### 2. Size

The diameter of the ball shall not be less than 1.680 inches (42.67mm). This specification will be satisfied if, under its own weight, a ball falls through a 1.680 inches diameter ring gauge in fewer than 25 out of 100 randomly selected positions, the test being carried out at a temperature of 23 ± 1°C.

### 3. Spherical Symmetry

The ball must not be designed, manufactured or intentionally modified to have properties which differ from those of a spherically symmetrical ball.

### 4. Initial Velocity

The initial velocity of the ball shall not exceed the limit specified (test on file) when measured on apparatus approved by the United States Golf Association.

### 5. Overall Distance Standard

The combined carry and roll of the ball, when tested on apparatus approved by the United States Golf Association, shall not exceed the distance specified under the conditions set forth in the Overall Distance Standard for golf balls on file with the United States Golf Association.

# RULES OF
# AMATEUR STATUS

## *Rules of Amateur Status*

Any person who considers that any action he is proposing to take might endanger his amateur status should submit particulars to the United States Golf Association for consideration.

### Definition of an Amateur Golfer

An amateur golfer is one who plays the game as a non-remunerative or non-profit-making sport.

**Rule 1**    **Forfeiture of Amateur Status at Any Age**

The following are examples of acts at any age which are contrary to the Definition of an Amateur Golfer and cause forfeiture of amateur status:

1. **Professionalism**

   a. Receiving payment or compensation for serving as a professional golfer or identifying oneself as a professional golfer.

   b. Taking any action for the purpose of becoming a professional golfer.

   **Note:** Such actions include applying for a professional's position; filing an application to a school or competition conducted to qualify persons to play as professionals in tournaments; directly or indirectly receiving services or payment from a professional agent or sponsor, commercial or otherwise; directly or indirectly entering into a written or oral agreement with a professional agent or sponsor, commercial or otherwise; agreement to accept payment or compensation for allowing one's name or likeness as a skilled golfer to be used for any commercial purpose; and applying for, holding or retaining membership in any organization of professional golfers.

## 2. Playing for Prize Money

Playing for prize money or its equivalent in a match, tournament or exhibition.

**Note:** A player may participate in an event in which prize money or its equivalent is offered, provided that prior to participation he irrevocably waives his right to accept prize money in that event. (See USGA Policy on Gambling for definition of prize money.)

## 3. Instruction

Receiving payment or compensation, directly or indirectly, for giving instruction in playing golf, either orally, in writing, by pictures or by other demonstrations, to either individuals or groups.

**Exceptions:**

1. Golf instruction may be given by an employee of an educational institution or system to students of the institution or system and by camp counselors to those in their charge, provided that the total time devoted to golf instruction during a year comprises less than 50 percent of the time spent during the year in the performance of all duties as such employee or counselor.

2. Payment or compensation may be accepted for instruction in writing, provided one's ability or reputation as a golfer was not a major factor in one's employment or in the commission or sale of one's work.

4. **Prizes, Testimonials and Gifts**

   a. Acceptance of a prize or testimonial of the following character (this applies to total prizes received for any event or series of events in any one tournament or exhibition, including hole-in-one or other events in which golf skill is a factor):

      (i) Of retail value exceeding $500; or

      (ii) Of a nature which is the equivalent of money or makes it readily convertible into money.

      **Exceptions:**

      1. Prizes of only symbolic value (such as metal trophies).

      2. More than one testimonial award may be accepted from different donors even though their total retail value exceeds $500, provided they are not presented so as to evade the $500 value limit for a single award. (Testimonial awards relate to notable performances or contributions to golf, as distinguished from tournament prizes.)

   b. Conversion of a prize into money.

   c. Accepting expenses in any amount as a prize.

   d. Because of golf skill or golf reputation, accepting in connection with any golfing event:

      (i) Money, or

      (ii) Anything else, other than merchandise of nominal value provided to all players.

5. **Lending Name or Likeness**

   Because of golf skill or golf reputation, receiving

or contracting to receive payment, compensation or personal benefit, directly or indirectly, for allowing one's name or likeness as a golfer to be used in any way for the advertisement or sale of anything, whether or not used in or appertaining to golf, except as a golf author or broadcaster as permitted by Rule 1-7.

6. **Personal Appearance**

Because of golf skill or golf reputation, receiving payment or compensation, directly or indirectly, for a personal appearance, except that reasonable expenses actually incurred may be received if no golf competition or exhibition is involved.

7. **Broadcasting and Writing**

Because of golf skill or golf reputation, receiving payment or compensation, directly or indirectly, for broadcasting concerning golf, a golf event or golf events, writing golf articles or books, or allowing one's name to be advertised or published as the author of golf articles or books of which one is not actually the author.

**Exceptions:**

1. Broadcasting or writing as part of one's primary occupation or career, provided instruction in playing golf is not included except as permitted in Rule 1-3.

2. Part-time broadcasting or writing, provided (a) the player is actually the author of the commentary, articles or books, (b) instruction in playing golf is not included except as permitted in Rule 1-3 and (c) the payment or compensation does not

have the purpose or effect, directly or indirectly, of financing participation in a golf competition or golf competitions.

8. **Golf Equipment**

   Because of golf skill or golf reputation, accepting golf balls, clubs, golf merchandise, golf clothing or golf shoes, directly or indirectly, from anyone manufacturing such merchandise without payment of current market price.

9. **Membership and Privileges**

   Because of golf skill or golf reputation, accepting membership or privileges in a club or at a course without full payment for the class of membership involved.

   **Exception:** Membership or privileges may be accepted provided that they have been awarded (1) as purely and deservedly honorary, (2) in recognition of an outstanding performance or contribution to golf, (3) without any time limit and (4) at no charge to anyone.

10. **Expenses**

    Accepting expenses, in money or otherwise, from any source other than from a member of the player's family or legal guardian to engage in a golf competition or exhibition, or to improve golf skill.

    **Exceptions:** A player may receive a reasonable amount of expenses as follows:

    **1. Age Restrictions**

    As a player in any amateur golf competition or exhibition or to improve golf skill until (i) the

September 1 following graduation from secondary school or (ii) his 19th birthday, whichever shall come first.

## 2. Team Competitions

As a representative of a recognized golf club or golf association in a team practice session (within limits fixed by the USGA) and/or team competition between or among golf clubs or golf associations when such expenses are paid by one or more of the golf clubs or golf associations involved or, subject to the approval of the USGA, as a representative in a team competition conducted by some other athletic organization.

## 3. USGA Public Links Championships

As a qualified contestant in the USGA Amateur Public Links Championships proper, but only within limits fixed by the USGA.

## 4. School, College, Military Teams

As a representative of a recognized educational institution or of a military service in (1) team events or (2) other events which are limited to representatives of recognized educational institutions or of military services, respectively. In each case, expenses may be accepted from only an educational or military authority.

## 5. Industrial or Business Teams

As a representative of an industrial or business golf team in industrial or business golf team competitions, respectively, but only within limits fixed by the USGA. (A statement of such limits may be obtained on request from the USGA.)

### 6. Invitation Unrelated to Golf Skill

As a player invited for reasons unrelated to golf skill (e.g., a celebrity, a business associate or customer, a guest in a club-sponsored competition, a winner of a random drawing, etc.) to take part in a golf event or to improve golf skill.

**Note 1:** Except as otherwise provided in the Exceptions to Rule 1-10, acceptance of expenses from an employer, a partner or other vocational source is not permissible.

**Note 2:** Business Expenses—It is permissible to play in a golf competition while on a business trip with expenses paid provided that the golf part of the expenses is borne personally and is not charged to business. Further, the business involved must be actual and substantial, and not merely a subterfuge for legitimizing expenses when the primary purpose is golf competition.

**Note 3:** Private Transport—Acceptance of private transport furnished or arranged for by a tournament sponsor, directly or indirectly, as an inducement for a player to engage in a golf competition or exhibition shall be considered accepting expenses under Rule 1-10.

### 11. Scholarships

Because of golf skill or golf reputation, accepting the benefits of a scholarship or grant-in-aid other than in accord with the regulation of the National Collegiate Athletic Association, the Association of Intercollegiate Athletics for Women, the National Association for Intercollegiate Athletics, the

National Junior College Athletic Association, or other similar organizations governing athletes at academic institutions.

### 12. Conduct Detrimental to Golf

Any conduct, including activities in connection with golf gambling, which is considered detrimental to the best interests of the game.

## Rule 2. Advisory Opinions, Enforcement and Reinstatement

### 1. Advisory Opinions

Any person who considers that any action he is proposing to take might endanger his amateur status may submit particulars to the staff of the United States Golf Association for advice. If dissatisfied with the staff's advice, he may request that the matter be referred to the Amateur Status and Conduct Committee for decision. If dissatisfied with the Amateur Status and Conduct Committee's decision, he may, by written notice to the staff within 30 days after being notified of the decision, appeal to the Executive Committee, in which case he shall be given reasonable notice of the next meeting of the Executive Committee at which the matter may be heard and shall be entitled to present his case in person or in writing. The decision of the Executive Committee shall be final.

### 2. Enforcement

Whenever information of a possible act contrary to the Definition of an Amateur Golfer by a player claiming to be an amateur shall come to the attention of the United States Golf Association, the staff shall notify the player of the possible act contrary to the Definition of an Amateur Golfer, invite the player to submit such information as the player deems relevant and make such other investigation as seems appropriate under the circumstances. The staff shall submit to the Amateur Status and Conduct Committee all information provided by the player, their findings and their recommendation, and the Amateur Status and Conduct Committee shall decide whether an act contrary to the Definition of an Amateur Golfer has occurred. If dissatisfied with the Amateur Status and Conduct Committee's decision, the player may, by written notice to the staff within 30 days after being notified of the decision, appeal to the Executive Committee, in which case the player shall be given reasonable notice of the next meeting of the Executive Committee at which the matter may be heard and shall be entitled to present his case in person or in writing. The decision of the Executive Committee shall be final.

Upon a final decision of the Amateur Status and Conduct Committee or the Executive Committee that a player has acted contrary to the Definition of an Amateur Golfer, such Committee may require the player to refrain or desist from specified actions as a condition of retaining his amateur status or declare the amateur status of the player forfeited. Such Committee shall notify the player, if possible, and may notify any interested golf association of any action taken under this paragraph.

3. **Reinstatement**

a. **Authority and Principles**

Either the Executive Committee or its Amateur Status and Conduct Committee may reinstate a player to amateur status and prescribe the waiting period necessary for reinstatement or deny reinstatement. In addition, the Amateur Status and Conduct Committee may authorize the staff of the USGA to reinstate a player to amateur status and prescribe the waiting period necessary for reinstatement in situations where the acts contrary to the Definition of an Amateur Golfer are covered by ample precedent.

Each application for reinstatement shall be decided on its merits with consideration normally being given to the following principles:

(i) Awaiting Reinstatement: The professional holds an advantage over the amateur by reason of having devoted himself to the game as his profession; other persons acting contrary to the Rules of Amateur Status also obtain advantages not available to the amateur. They do not necessarily lose such advantage merely by deciding to cease acting contrary to the Rules.

Therefore, an applicant for reinstatement to amateur status shall undergo a period awaiting reinstatement as prescribed.

The period awaiting reinstatement shall start from the date of the player's last act contrary to the Definition of an

Amateur Golfer unless it is decided that it shall start from the date of the player's last known act contrary to the Definition of an Amateur Golfer.

(ii) Period Awaiting Reinstatement: A period awaiting reinstatement of two years normally will be required. However, that period may be extended or shortened. Longer periods normally will be required when applicants have played extensively for prize money, regardless of performance, or have been previously reinstated; shorter periods often will be permitted when applicants have acted contrary to the Rules for one year or less. A probationary period of one year normally will be required when an applicant's only act contrary to the Definition of an Amateur Golfer was to accept a prize of retail value exceeding $500.

(iii) Players of National Prominence: Players of national prominence who have acted contrary to the Definition of an Amateur Golfer for more than five years normally will not be eligible for reinstatement.

(iv) Status During Period Awaiting Reinstatement: During the period awaiting reinstatement an applicant for reinstatement shall conform with the Definition of an Amateur Golfer.

He shall not be eligible to enter competitions limited to amateurs except that he may enter competitions solely among members of a club of which he is a member, subject to the approval of the club. He may also, without prejudicing his application, enter, as an applicant for reinstatement, competitions which are not limited to amateurs but shall not accept any prize reserved for an amateur.

### b. Form of Application

Each application for reinstatement shall be prepared, in duplicate, on forms provided by the USGA.

The application must be filed through a recognized amateur golf association in whose district the applicant resides. The association's recommendation, if any, will be considered. If the applicant is unknown to the association, this should be noted and the application forwarded to the USGA, without prejudice.

### c. Objection by Applicant

If dissatisfied with the decision with respect to his application for reinstatement, the applicant may, by written notice to the staff within 30 days after being notified of the decision, appeal to the Executive Committee, in which case he shall be given reasonable notice of the next meeting of the Executive Committee at which the matter may be heard and shall be entitled to present his case in person or in writing. The decision of the Executive Committee shall be final.

## *USGA Policy on Gambling*

The Definition of an Amateur Golfer provides that an amateur golfer is one who plays the game as a non-remunerative or non-profit-making sport. When gambling motives are introduced, problems can arise which threaten the integrity of the game.

The USGA does not object to participation in wagering among individual golfers or teams of golfers when participation in the wagering is limited to the players, the players may only wager on themselves or their teams, the sole source of all money won by players is advanced by the players and the primary purpose is the playing of the game for enjoyment.

The distinction between playing for prize money and gambling is essential to the validity of the Rules of Amateur Status. Participation in wagering among individual golfers and participation in wagering among teams constitutes golf wagering and not playing for prize money.

On the other hand, organized amateur events open to the general golfing public and designed and promoted to create cash prizes are not approved by the USGA. Golfers participating in such events without irrevocably waiving their right to cash prizes are deemed by the USGA to be playing for prize money.

The USGA is opposed to and urges its Member Clubs, all golf associations and all other sponsors of golf competitions to prohibit types of gambling such as: (1) Calcuttas, (2) other auction pools, (3) pari-mutuels and (4) any other forms of gambling organized for general participation or permitting participants to bet on someone other than themselves or their teams.

The Association may deny amateur status, entry in USGA Championships and membership on USGA teams for international competitions to players whose activities in connection with golf gambling, whether organized or individual, are considered by the USGA to be contrary to the best interests of golf.

# *INDEX*
# *TO THE*
# *RULES OF GOLF*

# *Index to the Rules of Golf*

## NOTES

## NOTES